I0002872

Fontographer

Practical Font Design
For Graphic Designers

Fontographer™

Practical
Font Design
For Graphic
Designers

David Bergsland

Written and published in September, 2011
© David Bergsland • All Rights Reserved
ISBN-13: 978-1466479401

ISBN-10: 146647940X

Mankato, Minnesota • http://radiqx.com • info@radiqx.com

Please let us know if there is anyway I can help you with your font design or publishing endeavors.

I refuse to take part in the legalistic trademark game. My guess is that this first mention should have Fontographer® or maybe even FontLab Fontographer®. I know that it is legally the *Adobe* Creative Suite®, but we all call it the Creative Suite or just CS. The same is true of *Aldus* PageMaker®, *Aldus* FreeHand®, *Macromedia* FreeHand®, and *Adobe* FreeHand®, *Adobe* InDesign®, *Adobe* Illustrator® (AI), *Adobe* Photoshop®, Quark*XPress*®, and many more. So, I just use PageMaker, FreeHand, Quark, InDesign, Illustrator, and Photoshop—probably *Adobe* Acrobat *Pro*® too. Surely you all know these things and I just want to talk with you in normal language about our common experiences. So, if you ever see all of this stuff added to these books, know that I have been attacked by lawyers.

*I dedicate this to my best friend
& soul mate, Pastor Pat
& the Lord whom we both serve—
who has adopted us
into the Chosen People whom we love*

Contents

Fontographer or FontLab?

We need to get this question out of the way before we get started. Personally, I started in Fontographer in the early 1990s and gradually built a little sideline of designing fonts. They were selling a little on Myfonts.

When OpenType became viable with the release of InDesign I needed to find something else. My old version of Fontographer would not run in Mac OSX very well. Thomas Phinney, then of Adobe, told me I had no option but to go to FontLab. This transformed my career. I learned how to write OpenType features. I learned how to carefully and professionally hand space fonts. I learned an entirely new way of drawing that was necessitated by FontLab's tools. It was eight years of hard work.

I wrote about what I learned in a book called *Practical Font Design*. It was and is still surprisingly popular. Earlier this year Ted Harrison, president of FontLab, contacted me to see if I was interested in bundling *Practical Font Design* with his software and possibly writing a version of *Practical Font Design* for Fontographer. I was and am grateful for the opportunity. Plus, I was really looking forward to relearning Fontographer, now in version 5.1.

Which one should you use?

It depends on your background. People like myself will probably continue to use both. Fontographer for drawing and FontLab for the more technical portions.

Fontographer

Fontographer is for people like myself with a long history of drawing with Bézier curves and working in typography. Because FreeHand was developed out of Fontographer, Free-Hand experience is good. Illustrator and InDesign experience also translates well. This is a superb drawing program for typographers who want to take the next step.

Fontographer is a wonderful drawing experience. It has been a real joy to experience that fun again. After nearly a decade in FontLab, font design is fun again.

There are some limitations. Adding the character slots for Eastern European, Cyrillic, or Hebrew characters would be a real pain, for example, without an existing sample font. Fontographer cannot write OpenType feature files. You cannot show the names of characters in the font window unless they are Unicode glyphs—and characters for oldstyle figures, small caps, small cap figures, denominators, and so on do not have Unicode names. Its hand letterspacing tools are really laborious and difficult to control. But that is compensated for by the power of its Auto Space and Auto Kern controls. Fontographer does a good job of auto spacing.

Fontographer is for digital graphic designers who need to make or edit fonts in the course of their work.

FontLab

FontLab is a professional font design program for people who went to school to learn font design and people working in the font industry. Its interface is not nearly so intuitive as Fontographer, but it is much more powerful. You can control it with Python scripts, you can write OpenType features within it. It can do class-based kerning easily and well. It has a far superior interface for people who need to hand produce all the letterspacing and kerning in a font.

It does really well at generating new glyphs for special encodings. It can automatically add any new glyphs used by an OpenType feature set, use multiple master fonts for building font families, work with up to 64,000 characters (for Asian fonts), right-to-left (Arabic and Hebrew) text support, programmable font transformation, encoding templates, editing CMap files, manual TrueType and Type 1 hinting, and test fonts with Font Auditor. Plus it can show character names in the font window.

FontLab is for the professional font designer and others who need to create robust, commercial-quality fonts

Acknowledgements

In a forty year career like mine, there are too many people to mention all who helped me on my way. The major change came when I met the Lord in 1974. He moved me gently off my self-centered fine art trip into creating beauty as a service in what was then called commercial art.

Some of the people who helped in that change must be mentioned, first and foremost my wife, Patricia, who encouraged and supported me in my lunacy. My first art director, Pik in West Virginia 1979, was a huge inspiration. I had never before seen a man who could toss off marker roughs where the type was so accurate you could take measurements off it—all drawn as fast as a graffiti scribbler. That's where my love of typography and typographic illustration began.

Actually, my love of typography was birthed in my Far Eastern art history classes under the enthusiasm of Dr. Robert Poor at the University of Minnesota in the late 60s and early 70s. It was a real revelation to learn about a culture which considered calligraphy a higher art form than painting.

As I entered the digital age, the books of Robin Williams, Sandee Cohen, Ole Kvern, and Roger Black were a great help as well as Bringhurst, Spiekermann, and Cabarga. Thomas Phinney took the time to write me, answer questions, and encourage me as I began to get serious about font design as did Allan Haley. In the book I tell of the influence of Colin Brignall at Letraset as I began my journey toward font design by cutting PMT enlargements of transfer lettering into pieces to be rearranged into typographic designs.

Richard Fink was the first to give the original book a serious review, and he has helped me a lot with this one. His feedback, questions, and commentary gave me a much better sense of the different needs of various users—especially as far as hinting and Web fonts are concerned. Then of course, there's his enthusiasm and drive. He's been fun to work with in this book.

I can't forget all my students, especially Marcia Best, Lois Bradley, and Adam Baney among many others. Adam was the first to push me toward writing what became *Practical Font Design* (though he's been too busy to take the course which resulted from his questions. Hopefully the book meets that need in a small way).

Michael Kleper at RIT took the time to make some editing suggestions that were very helpful. They helped me clarify my perspective and stance for this looser style of book. I'm trying to avoid the tense legalism and absence of opinion necessary for academia—though I do confess that many of his comments showed where I had just gone too far.

Ted Harrison of FontLab was the direct impetus behind this book on Fontographer. I am thankful for the gentle request and I am grateful for the opportunity to get back to the software that started it all for me. There are many more whom I am thankful for, but it's time to get into the book...

October 18, 2001

Who is this book written for?

Fontographer is an application which appeals to experienced graphics designers with a background in PostScript illustration—especially those with (Altsys, Aldus, or Macromedia) FreeHand experience from version 7 and earlier. This vector drawing program set the standard for ease of use and innovation in the early days of digital design. The near majority of designers working in the mid-1990s had a copy of Fontographer. It came free with the FreeHand Graphics Studio first released in 1995—and more than 50,000 designers used Fontographer because of it [at least a little].

Fontographer had [and still has] a unique and intuitive set of drawing tools that enable amateurs of that era to enter the world of font design. I'm talking amateurs in the sense that John Baskerville considered himself an amateur—as I also consider myself, though I am certainly not in Baskerville's league. For me, font design is a beloved sideline with which I indulge myself. It's become a treasured tool I use in my current trade—book writing, designing, and production.

What about younger designers?

There are a couple of problems.
First are the actual drawing skills required.

The good news here is that Fontographer is easy to learn and quick to comprehend. Its drawing tools can be added to your creative repertoire in a few weeks. This is especially true for simple designs like sans serif fonts. But if you work hard you can draw almost any kind of font because the actual letter shapes are relatively simple.

The problem is seen in the sophistication of those simple shapes. A circle or a point does not stop at the measurement lines but goes slightly beyond them to produce those optical adjustments which are absolutely essential to make these simple shapes line up along the lines of letters and words that make up a sentence, paragraph, and column of type. Though many 21st century designers appear to destroy the old rules, we typographers know that the actual appearance of freedom from antiquated rules is very difficult to achieve while maintaining the readability which content requires for communication.

This brings us to the second problem: typography

I blithely tossed in the term typographer in the last sentence. That simple term is not commonly understood or comprehended today. In addition, moving along the path from typesetter to typographer takes time. Study is required. Experience is essential. This is not something that can be entered into lightly or easily. (Well, I take that back. It is commonly entered lightly and easily with disastrous results. Examples of incredibly ineffective typography are easy to find and exceedingly common. I am just so glad to know you are not listed among those design anarchists and contemporary cultural terrorists.)

Experience can be acquired quite quickly with a lot of study and diligent effort. Within just a few years, you can be producing gorgeous type designs. But you will need to work at it. You will need to immerse yourself into this tiny niche of design. The result of that amount of intense focus and effort might move part of your font production over into FontLab. But more about that potential turn of events after we learn about Fontographer.

What I expect from you

Fontographer appeals to people like myself who have been graphic designers and typographers for years, using the normal tools of the printing trades: what is now known as the Creative Suite [InDesign (out of PageMaker), Illustrator, & Photoshop] plus Quark, FreeHand, and Acrobat.

You love type. You regularly tear apart letters and words to build logos and typographic art. You are comfortable with the Pen tool, composite paths, and drawing simple shapes. Font design is only concerned with simple black and white shapes. If you are one of these people, Fontographer is like going home.

This is especially true if you started this process back in the early 1990s as I did. You've always worked on a Mac (because PCs just couldn't do it until the last half of the 90s—it didn't support PostScript completely until XP). If you loved FreeHand, you'll love Fontographer. It will take some adjustments. If you are coming from Illustrator, it will be a more difficult adjustment. (There has never been a need for the Direct Selection tool, as a simple example.) There are no custom keyboard shortcuts, fancy toolbars, or customizable interface to be found here.

Fontographer is a lean, fast software application: It launches in a couple seconds. It has twenty tools and you will only be using fifteen of them (or less, in most cases). There are fewer than two dozen menu commands and shortcuts to learn. This is a very fast, easy to understand, and quick to use drawing tool. But the drawing experience, once you fit yourself within its elegant paradigm, is excellent.

Fontographer is clean, quick, elegant, and most importantly FUN!

This has been the most important revelation as I have returned to Fontographer these past few months. Drawing has become fun again. After years of effort and decades of experience, much of the clean simple fun that motivated me in the beginning had been buried in the complexity of work. Fontographer broke me free from that, making creativity fun again—as I haven't experienced it for a long time.

If you do not have the experience

You can still experience a great deal of fun as you produce your fonts. It will probably take you quite bit longer to get control of what you are doing, to understand what is required, and to come to know yourself well enough to express that knowledge with a design that really satisfies.

Fontographer is a great design tool and its simplicity will not get in the way as you learn about letter shapes and how they are put together. It will definitely help you in the conversion process from typesetter to typographer. Achieving excellence always takes work and dedication. But the tool itself will not get in your way. You will be free to learn and grow in skill as you become a font designer.

The key role of Fontographer in the font revolution

The world of font design has radically changed in the digital world of graphic design. We no longer make huge careful drawings, reduced to perfection, and exquisitely carved out of metal or exposed onto film. We make mathematically precise, infinitely editable, completely resizable shapes output as code.

The software that brought about that change is the focus of this book: Fontographer. The major change in the type design industry happened earlier with much more expensive proprietary digital systems. But for us it happened when Macromedia released FreeHand Graphics Studio—a bundle with FreeHand 5.5, XRes, Extreme 3D, and Fontographer 4. By the time the Graphics Studio that came with FreeHand 7 came out, FreeHand was approaching its peak of popularity with well over 200,000 users. The Graphics Studio gave large numbers of eager, newly digital, graphic designers a wonderfully easy and intuitive tool for designing fonts. Most of us at least played with it. If you knew FreeHand, Fontographer was obvious and easy to use.

Fontographer was a revelation. Few knew this was the program that started it all as far as we were concerned. It was the first PostScript illustration program with its release in January 1986 by Altsys, with version 2.0 coming out in the fall of 1986. Illustrator was not released until January 1987. FreeHand came out in 1988 as a further development of Fontographer into a complete drawing program.

With the vagaries surrounding FreeHand's demise as it traveled from Altsys to Aldus and back to Altsys with Adobe's purchase of Aldus then on to Macromedia (under governmental anti-trust pressure) to its death at the hands of Adobe when it was purchased again, Fontographer was left alone and simply became a standard that "everyone had" in their arsenal. FontLab purchased the rights to it. The application was left alone even as it suffered by being left behind without an upgrade to the new world of Mac OSX at the beginning of the new millennium.

The good news: Fontographer 5.1 has been worth the wait

Many of us were excited when FontLab purchased Fontographer in the Spring of 2005. An OSX-compatible version with no changes to the interface was released in 2006. Finally a new version, Fontographer 5, was released in June 2010. This book is being written using the new Fontographer 5.1 which has been rewritten for the most recent OSX, Lion, which will no longer support Rosetta and the PowerPC applications.

Hundreds, even thousands, of new font designers

What Fontographer did was add many new designers to the font world. When I was given the opportunity to write my first textbook on the all-digital printing workflow in 1994, I used Fontographer to design all the fonts I used in that book. I was frustrated with the lack of true small caps and lowercase figures in the common text fonts available in that day. I designed the Diaconia family, based on Minister. Plus, I created NuevoLitho, a radically loosened C&lc version of Lithos, for the heads. My font design career took off when I was contacted by Makambo and asked if I wanted to offer my fonts for sale through them. My experiences with the thievery surrounding shareware fonts led me to try that. When Bitstream started MyFonts (absorbing Makambo in the process), they asked me to offer my fonts with them.

I found a satisfying new source of income along with the creative outlet.

Fontographer is almost certainly at least partially responsible for the huge growth in the number of font designers. At one time, there were upwards of 50,000 Fontographer users. Even though there are only a couple hundred members in the professional type designers' groups like ATypI and TypeCon, Fonts.com (Monotype) currently shows 1751 designers. MyFonts lists 1268 foundries, many of whom have several or even many designers. This does not include the thousands of graphic designers who have modified a font for their own use and/or made a partial font.

I'm just a typographer and graphic designer who loves type. I am very much an outsider to the font industry. My experience is that font designers are a wonderfully individualistic group of people—though there is certainly a huge amount of pompous poopery.

Our only shared attributes are a love of type, typesetting, typography, and strong opinions. But our differences stand out in that we cannot even find a common definition of the word typography. All of this is coupled with the fact that typographers are an esoteric and inconspicuous niche of a relatively small trade. Our concerns are virtually unknown outside the industry.

This is an evolving on-demand book

That means that I can continuously update the artwork as typos are found. Radiqx Press and Hackberry Font Foundry are very low budget operations, so I have done everything possible to keep the cost of production low to keep your costs low.

The book is in response to several requests

With the success of my *Practical Font Design* book for FontLab, I have been made aware of the need for a book on the one that started it all, Fontographer. This is the application which gave me a new career and changed my typography.

As I've said, this little book gives me the chance to go back to my roots, as it were, and regain some of the fun I had at first. I have been pleasantly surprised at how much joy I have found going back to the clean, clear drawing interface that started it all. I had been thinking that I really missed FreeHand—especially the older versions. Actually, I've missed Fontographer, the app that came first—far before Illustrator.

> **Beware!**
> This will not be a neat, tidy book with a logical progression of easily understood steps toward the finished font. My experience is that font design is a constantly evolving, ever changing process. What I plan to do is allow you to get inside my head (as much as I can) so you can see the thought processes you will go through as you design your fonts—sharing things you need to consider.
>
> Hopefully, you will find this helpful. My goal is to free you up to be creative fluidly without worrying about all the changes in direction and design that are inevitable in a project like this.

In addition, as I talk about things I need for my designs I will make those pieces available to you on my Website: hackberry-fonts.com. I expected that there would be much to learn as I went back to drawing fonts, as opposed to assembling fonts. What surprised me was the joy. Font design had become work. Like most teaching ventures, I'm sure I learned as much as you will if you follow through the book.

The best way to learn from this book

Design your own font as we go through step-by-step

My hope is that as you read about my thought processes they will enable you to make your personal response to them by designing a font of your own. If you find things missing, please let me know. First of all, I will answer any questions you have. Second, I will update the book, giving you credit, and give you a free copy of the new ebook versions: david@bergsland.org will do it.

Welcome!

...to an experiment in font design

Not a horribly auspicious way to start out a book is it? It is the way I start out my FontLab book, but things have changed since then. I had lost my experimental, creative edge—entering into font production as a career. Now after writing this book, I find that I really do not like font design as a career (writing and book design do that for me), but I still love it as a creative expression.

Nevertheless, it is still an experiment. All of my font designs are experiments. Honestly, as a font designer, my only credentials are experience and practice tied to a growing body of customers who have purchased my experiments. Since going full-time with Hackberry Font Foundry and the Radiqx Press publishing house in 2009 I have learned a lot.

Mainly I have learned that my personal vision is simply that—personal. I am not claiming superiority to anyone. In fact, I am an amateur in the old British sense of the word. I'm really into it. I've gotten quite experienced. But I have no interest in what the industry says must be done. Most of the modern fashionable font designs seem far too overdone and nearly pretentious to my eye. Showing off is for kids. My focus is simply on getting good fonts I can use and which meet my needs. They are designed as simply and easily as possible. I am merely sharing what I have learned as an alternative to design school training. For me, self-taught is not a hostile epithet but a way of life.

Corinthian Light

ABCDEFGHIJ
KLMNOPQR
STUVWXYZ
1234567890
abcdefghijklmn
opqrstuvwxyz

Created by Letraset Type Director Colin Brignall, this clean-cut, monolineal sans serif typeface was inspired by Edward Johnston's Railway Type and Eric Gill's Gill Sans typefaces.

Defining typography

What's unusual is that none of the dictionaries really get it. They describe the physical act, but typography really has little to do with the physical act of arranging letters on paper for printing. Obviously physical considerations and traditional shapes play a huge role in type design. But typography goes far beyond the actual shapes into the cultural and subjective responses of individual readers.

Here's what the dictionaries understand about the craft

- ❦ Webster's: The craft of composing type and printing from it; art and technique of printing with movable type.

- ❦ Random House: the art or process of printing with type; the work of setting and arranging types and of printing from them; the general character or appearance of printed matter

- ❦ Wikipedia: art of arranging letters on a page to be printed, usually for a combination of aesthetic and functional goals

Wikipedia does the best job. What we are about is directing those responses with our art and our craft. My focus in this book is that craft we call font design used for the art of typography on a professional level.

Quotations on typography

There are countless quotes from people in our craft that hit more directly on the true purpose and focus of typography. Here are a few of them to help us get started.

As an aside: For poetic beauty, no one has ever described the role of type, fonts, and typography better than Bringhurst in the foreword of his standard, *The Elements of Typographic Style*

> Type appears at first to be a rigid medium; but like other rigid media, it is plastic to the living spirit of a craftsman.   J.H. MASON, BRIAR PRESS

Typography is directing a message.
GÜNTER GERHARD LANGE

In all arts the belief in counting and measuring
leads to the greatest mistakes.   PAUL RENNER

Good typography explains the content, not the
designer.   KURT WEIDEMANN

Not surprisingly, the best quote is from Hermann Zapf

Typography is two-dimensional architecture, based
on experience and imagination, and guided by
rules and readability. And this is the purpose of
typography: The arrangement of design elements
within a given structure should allow the reader to
easily focus on the message, without slowing down
the speed of his reading.

My definition is simple:
Typography is the art of communicating clearly and easily with type

All humans need to believe that they as individuals
are important. We commonly see typography as a worthy
focus of our life. It is common for us to see typography as
part of the foundation of our culture. I believe that myself.
But there is no reason for the pomposity commonly seen in
typographic opinion. Important we are. Civilization & culture
would be lessened without our skill. Understood we are not.
Influential? Not hardly.

The result of all of this is a plethora of strongly stated
opinions that rarely agree. They are expressed by people who
commonly segregate themselves into little cliques, schools,
and movements. My position is that of insignificant outsider.
The best I can offer is my attempt in this book to be an
objective reporter of my knowledge and experiences. I can
only hope you find this useful. It will certainly be useful to
me as I continue in my career as a full time author, typographer, and font designer. I expect to come out of this at the

end of the book a much more informed designer. Hopefully, that will translate into better designs.

What you can reasonably expect

A starting point from which you can realistically decide if type design is for you. There are many reasons why this may not be for you. Type design is intricate, complicated, tedious, individualistic, opinionated, intellectual, emotional, objective, subjective, and so on. It is entirely self-motivated. It is not pursued for monetary reward [well, not much anyway].

It will be a voyage of discovery for me. I hope you find it entertaining. In the original book, I discovered things I was not aware of like it is now obvious to me that a major influence on my design style and taste is Colin Brignall, the Type Director for Letraset in the 1970s and '80s. In looking for fonts to show in the sidebar I simply started showing fonts that I love. The first three I wanted to show in the original book were all designed by Colin. But then, my formative years typographically were spent dissecting and reworking headlines and subheads produced with presstype. I found that for me the only presstype worth using was Letraset. So I shouldn't be surprised. But I've just been too busy setting type and designing fonts to notice before.

This font is Romic which I used as the inspiration for the font designed for the FontLab version of *Practical Font Design*. It's one of those fonts I've always loved, but rarely used. I never found a client who could handle it. Now that I have the freedom to use it , I use

Romic Light

ABCDEFGHIJ
KLMNOPQR
STUVWXYZ
1234567890

abcdefghijkl
mnopqrstuv
wxyz

Designed by Colin Brignall in 1979 for Letraset, Romic is based on pen-formed letters and was created to offer a new approach to serif design that would allow for close spacing of text.

my own fonts. So, Romic is just a font with good associa-
tions for me even though I've never actually used it.

The font I ended up with in that original book as
Aromé Oldstyle was finally released as Ablati, with a fun
italic. The only real tie to Romic was the asymmetrical serifs.

ABCDEFGHIJKL
MNOPQRSTUV
WXYZabcdefghi
jklmnopqrstuvw
xyz 1234567890
1234567890

Some type terminology

Before we press on, we need to cover some basic terms
so we can talk about the fonts and characters we will be
designing. The terminology is crucial to our discussion.

Type parts

Some terms you need to know are seen in the drawing
at the top of the next page. The baseline is the imaginary
line that all the letters and numbers sit on. The x-height
is the height of the lowercase x (the x is normally the only
lowercase letter that is flat both top and bottom). However,
I saw x-height called a mean line in a diagram on a typography Website the other day, although I have never actually
heard anyone use that term.

Ascenders are the portions of the lowercase letters that rise above the x-height as in b, d, f, h, k, and l. A t doesn't ascend far enough to be called an ascender, usually. Descenders are the portions that sink below the baseline as in g, j, p, q, and y. The cap height is the height of the uppercase letters.

Type terms & measurements

BUILT-IN LEADING (OPTIONAL FOR FONT DESIGNERS)

STEM

COUNTER
(OPEN AREA)

BOWL

BUILT-IN LEADING (OPTIONAL FOR FONT DESIGNERS)

Point Size
Ascender
Cap Height
X-Height
Optical Alignment Areas
Baseline
Descender
Point Size

The baseline, x-height and cap height are specified with optical alignment areas because curves have to extend over the lines to look the proper height. Yes, it is an optical illusion. The same is true of letters such as A or V that have points. If the point does not protrude past the guidelines, the letter looks obviously too short. Even people who know nothing about type will know that something is wrong. Type design has many of these understandings that have become fairly rigid rules.

If you look above, you will see that the x is the only character that fits the x-height for the font characters shown. You can even see that the serifs for the H overlap the baseline and cap height lines a little.

What I am calling the Optical Alignment Areas are commonly called the *overshoot*. You will discover that this optical alignment is crucial to excellence in typography. You need to even align the sides of the columns optically to make them seem straight, clean, and perfect. This puts the angled stems of an A or W outside the column edge. Only InDesign does that.

Revue

ABCDEFGHI JKLMNOPQR STUVWXYZ 1234567890

abcdefghij klmnopqrs tuvwxyz

Also designed by Colin Brignall in 1968 for Letraset, based on posters from the 1900s

Terms: You may have noticed that we just used two old letterpress terms. Those two terms are uppercase and lowercase. The original terms were majuscules for large letters and minuscules for handwriting using small letters. Majuscules came to be called capital letters. Minuscules remained a mouthful. Uppercase and lowercase come from common typesetting practice in hand-set letterpress where two wooden cases of letters were used in a standard setup. The upper case contained all the capital letters. The lower case contained all the minuscules. In other words, the common phrase caps and lower case (or C&lc) is just one of those things we do in English which drives people nuts.

Some glyph terminology

Before we get into classification specifics much later in the book, we need to define a few descriptive terms to help us talk about specific areas of a character or glyph as we design a font. The terms are a little esoteric, but I think you will find them helpful to categorize things in your own mind.

- Stems: the vertical strokes in letters like H, K, L, R, b, d, h, m, n and so on. An m has three stems.

- Bowls: the rounded parts of letters like B, D, G, O, P, b, d, g, and even C & S, according to some.

- Crossbars: the horizontal strokes on A, H, E, & so on.

- Arms: The horizontal bars at the top or bottom of a character like the E, F, & T.

- ❦ Head & Foot Serifs: the serifs at the top and bottom of a stem.

- ❦ Adnate Or Bracketed Serifs: serifs that flow smoothly (often gracefully) out of the stems.

- ❦ Abrupt Serifs: cross strokes at the end of stems with no bracketing.

- ❦ Terminals: the endings of the curved portions of letters like a, C, r, c, G, & so on.

- ❦ Lachrymal: terminals that are tear-drop shaped.

- ❦ Stroke: the lines that make up the characters from the old assumption that letters are calligraphic and drawn with separate strokes of a pen or brush.

- ❦ Modulated Stroke: a stroke that varies in width as it proceeds around the letter form.

- ❦ Axis: the angle the pen was held at to produce the modulated stroke of calligraphers.

- ❦ Humanist Axis: the axis for normal (bigoted?) right-handed calligraphic penmanship.

- ❦ Contrast: how much the stroke is modulated.

- ❦ Aperture: the openings of curves on letters like a, c, e, s, & so on.

- ❦ Slope: how far italic and oblique letters slant in degrees.

There are many more, but this will be enough for our purposes at this point. As you can see, type gets very technical. For some of you, the differences will seem insignificant now, as you learn type design. For many of you, these terms have been picked up over the years, but you never really had a definition.

They are really very important. Aperture, for example, tends to control the friendliness and readability. An axis change from humanist to mechanically vertical strongly influence our reaction to the warmness or coolness of a font. But we'll discuss these things as we go, giving you examples so you can see the differences.

Much of this is personal opinion

In terminology, as in all areas of font design, definitions and usage are a matter of who you talked too most recently. There really is no right or wrong, just different schools of thought. My goal is to define what I need to share so we can communicate. Hang around typophile.com and other type sites to increase your education.

How do you draw with paths?

This is the key to it all. Fontographer was the first PostScript drawing program—defining shapes via Bézier curves in a connect the dots manner. Fontographer works purely with the paths. No fancy extras. It doesn't even do "composite paths" per se—it simply controls path direction.

We'll get into the tools to create paths in a minute, but I felt it was essential to do a quick review of a path: how it is made, and why it works the way it does.

Fontographer has a really good basic set of drawing tools. Nothing fancy. But then fancy things cannot be included in fonts. Fonts require simple, black shapes.

Ideally, all shapes should be drawn as one continuous outline or path. Drawing short lines and connecting them is certainly possible. In fact that is easier in Fontographer than anywhere else. Regardless, all paths in a glyph must be closed (the endpoint on top of the start point).

Yes, this is basic review for many of you. But I am regularly amazed by how little experienced designers know about PostScript paths drawn with Bézier curves.

You use various tools to place points. The primary starting point is the Pen tool (which we'll cover in a bit). The points are placed in order around a shape & the path is produced by connecting them. These points are controlled by mathematical formulae to produce a path that can bend and change direction under direct control. These modifications are determined by point location & handles with control points. Each point has two handles.

Corner points, Curve points, & Handles

The following descriptions and definitions are almost certainly not accurate mathematically. *Who cares?* What is important is that they will help you understand how your paths work so you can control them. I have readers who are really into the mathematics, but the math does not help produce better looking design.

Start point:

This is where you begin your path. A path has a direction going from the first point to the second point and so on. In FontLab, the outside paths are drawn counter-clockwise by default. I use that convention in Fontographer in case my font file is ever edited in FontLab. But consistency is all that really matters.

Points:

These are the dots you place so that when mathematics controlling the code connects the dots a path is produced. Font characters do require points in specific locations called extrema which we will talk about in a bit.

Segments:

A segment is a portion of a path between two points. So, a segment is a straight line from point to point plus any length added by incoming or outgoing handles at the beginning or the end of the segment.

Handles:

These are tangent lines coming out of the points. A tangent is the straight line of the curve at that point (using the PostScript definition of a curve that is made up of very small straight line segments). Every segment has two handles: the outgoing handle toward the following point and an incoming handle toward the previous point. If a point appears to have no handles, or only a handle on one side of the point, the other handles simply have zero length. Zero length handles produce the shortest possible segment. If both the outgoing and incoming handles of a path segment have zero length, you have the shortest possible segment: a straight line from point to point. If the handle is aligned precisely with a straight line segment on either side of the point, its length does not affect the segment length (or curve the segment). Otherwise the handle determines the amount of curve.

Handle Control Points:

At the end of every handle is a small plus that can be grabbed with the mouse and moved to control the length & direction of the handle coming out of the point.

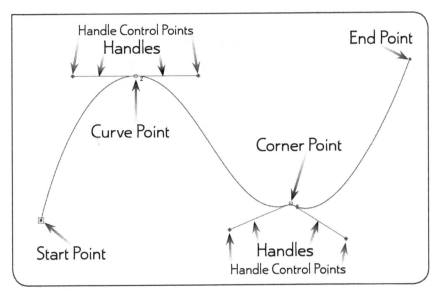

Corner points:

When these are produced by a click of the Pen tool, they have no handles—actually, no handles are visible. In fact, they have handles with no length. What that means is that paths coming into that point or going out from that point will go the shortest way possible—modified by the handle at the other end of the segment. If a corner point has visible handles, each of them can be moved independently.

Curve points:

When these are produced with a click-drag, they have handles of equal length that are locked onto a common tangent. This means if you move one handle, the other handle moves in an equal but opposite direction. If the curve handles have been modified in length they rotate around the point in opposite directions in proportion to the length of the handles involved. The common tangents make a smooth transition from one segment to the next.

Tangent points:

The handle attached to these points are locked onto the imaginary straight line segments to the preceding and following points on the path.

It will take a little practice

Points and handles seem very strange when you are just starting out. But you quickly become accustomed to them and rapidly begin to rely on them for precise, editable control of a shape.

Type drawing tools
The Fontographer Toolbox

If you see two little dots in the lower right corner of the tool, double-clicking the tool opens the Options or the Transform dialog box. These are what came to be known as the FreeHand tool set (up to FreeHand 8, anyway [when Macromedia joined the lemming march into complexity]).

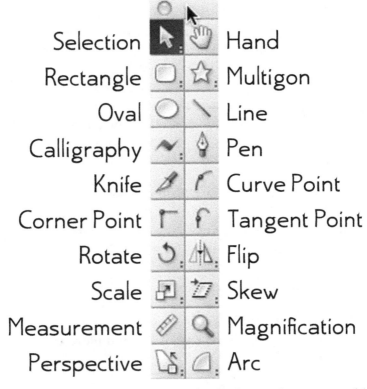

Selection	Hand
Rectangle	Multigon
Oval	Line
Calligraphy	Pen
Knife	Curve Point
Corner Point	Tangent Point
Rotate	Flip
Scale	Skew
Measurement	Magnification
Perspective	Arc

I am going to go through all the tools very quickly because these are the tools that set the standards for our everyday usage. Illustrator has messed things up (breaking simple tools into complex specializations). You do not need a round-cornered rectangle tool when all you need to do is double-click on the tool to set the radius (You need to do that in AI anyway). But as soon as you realize how clean and simple these tools are, they will become obvious to use. Remember, they are clean and easy to understand.

What a concept!

If you have come from FreeHand these will be a real joy! If you are coming from Illustrator, it will be a pleasant surprise and increasing joy that there are no hidden tools or complex specialized filters to remember or memorize.

Right-handed versus left-handed shortcuts

Fontographer does this better than most. Because most of the tools can be selected with a number, selecting tools can be easily done with the hand not holding the mouse as you work. Right-handed people can use the numbers on the QWERTY board. Lefties use the numbers on the numerical keypad. For lefties, this is one of the major benefits of a complete keyboard, plus because most of us are ambidextrous we can use either set of numbers with ease.

Selection tool [Shortcut: Grave (lowercase Tilde)]

This is the tool to select and edit paths and points. You use this to adjust handle positions of points. This shortcut is a major irritant to the left-handed. You either have to reach the whole way across the keyboard or drop the mouse. It's surprising how much this slows me down.

Hand tool [Shortcut: Spacebar]

It is used to grab the pasteboard and move everything around as needed.

Rectangle tool [Shortcut: One]

It draws rectangles. Hold down the shift and draw squares. Hold down the Option and draw from the center out. Hold down both to draw a square from the center out. Double-click for the dialog to control the corner radius. Individual corner control is not available.

Multigon tool [Shortcut: Two]

This is the star/polygon tool you wish you had in Illustrator. There is a slider for number of points in the polygon and a slider to adjust the acute to obtuse shape of the star points. But mainly **THERE IS A PREVIEW!** Of course, this begs the question: "When was the last time you drew a polygon or star anyway?"

Oval tool [Shortcut: Three]

It draws ovals. Hold down the shift and draw circles. Hold down the Option and draw from the center out.

Line tool [Shortcut: Four]

Draws straight lines. Hold down the shift key to constrain in 45° increments. Hold down the Option and draw from the center out.

Calligraphy Pen Tool [Shortcut: Five]

This does what you would expect—it mimics a flat nibbed fine art ink pen. Double-clicking gives you an option dialog box. You choose from a Pressure Sensitive pen controlled by a drawing tablet or a Calligraphic pen where you set the width and the angle to draw like you would with a flat nibbed pen.

Pen tool [Shortcut: Six]

The essence of simplicity. Click for a corner point. Click-drag for a curve point. The shift constrains the angle. The Option lets you drag handles out of placed corner points. To edit the path, hold down the Command key.

The reason it is so wonderful is that it never messes you up. If you command-click on the end point with the pen tool you can resume drawing and extending the path. If you select and delete a point, the path is broken at that point. To get rid of a point yet keep the path connected and/or closed, use the Merge Point command [Command+M]. Merging a point also smooths the curve nicely.

Merge endpoints: If you drop the endpoint of one path on top of the endpoint of another path, they merge into one point that connects the paths. This always seems to produce a corner point at that location, but you can merge it away or use the Command+8 shortcut to convert it to a curve point if necessary.

Knife tool [Shortcut: Seven]

Click on a path or drag across a path to cut the path. The shift key constrains the drag direction. It leaves the two new endpoints on top of each other.

Curve Point tool [Shortcut: Eight]

Click on a path to add a curve point. Select the endpoint of the path with the Selection tool and then click with the curve point tool to extend the path with a curve point or add a curve point wherever you need one on a path.

Corner Point tool [Shortcut: Nine]

Click on a path to add a corner point. Select the endpoint of the path with the Selection tool and then click with the corner point tool to extend the path with a corner point or to add a corner point wherever you need one. Corner points often do not have one or both of the handles showing. You can drag them out by selecting the point. Then you hold down the Option key and click-drag on the point to pull out the handle. The incoming handle is dragged out first. Remember that corner points with no handles really have two handles with zero length that can always be dragged out. You can retract the handles by typing Command+R.

Tangent Point tool [Shortcut: Zero]

Click on a path to add a tangent point. Select the endpoint of the path with the Selection tool and then click with the tangent point tool to extend the path with a tangent point. Tangent points were unique to Altsys. Adobe still does not use them (nor do I). They also have two handles like corner points. But the handles are locked onto an extension of the straight line between the tangent point and the preceding or following point.

Normally a tangent point only has one handle, coming out of a straight line segment on the other side of the point. To manipulate the other handle it is usually better to convert the tangent point to a curve point [Command+8] or corner point [Command+9] by typing the appropriate shortcut. Then it will be easier to drag out the missing handle with the Option key.

The transformation tools

These work differently than you expect, unless you have FreeHand experience. They transform around the click location. There is no transformational center. The further you move the mouse away from the click location, the more control you have over the transformation. They only take a little practice.

Rotate tool [No Shortcut]

Click and drag with the tool to rotate any selection around the location clicked. Move the mouse away from the click point for more control.

Flip tool [No Shortcut]

Click to flip the selection over the clicked location. Click-drag to rotate the flipped selection. For simple horizontal or vertical flips, it is often quicker and easier to type the shortcut for Transform [Command+\]. There you can have the dialog set up for horizontal, vertical, or both transforming around the center of the selection, the glyph origin point, the baseline point, or the last clicked location.

Scale tool [No Shortcut]

Click-drag to scale from the location clicked upon. Down-left at a 45° angle with make it smaller proportionally. Up-right at a 45° angle to make it larger proportionally.

Skew tool [No Shortcut]

Click-drag to skew from the location clicked upon.

Magnification tool [Shortcut: Command+Spacebar]

This is a normal Zoom tool. Click to enlarge. Option-click to reduce. Marquee to enlarge the marqueed area as large as possible.

Measurement tool [No Shortcut]

Click-drag to get a measurement in em units.

Perspective tool [No Shortcut]

Move the selected points in perspective. It is very confusing if you do not hold down the shift key to constrain the drag up, down, left or right. There's a good preview.

Arc tool [No Shortcut]

Click drag to draw a preselected arc. You choose the arc style by double-clicking on the tool to make your selection in the dialog box.

Vector drawing tools & techniques using Illustrator

As you might expect, drawing fonts digitally requires some unique skills. Most of you probably assume that this will be focused on Illustrator's pen tool. In many ways, that is a faulty assumption. While it is true that we will be working with PostScript paths, Illustrator does not have very good tools for simple path drawings.

I've really enjoyed getting back to the clean, simply path construction paradigm of Fontographer. Though it is true that Illustrator is the dominant vector drawing application, it is focused on fancy tools, techniques, and effects that cannot be used when drawing the very simple shapes of a font character. Though Adobe's pen tool works quite well, editing an Illustrator/InDesign path while you work on it has always been a real problem. This becomes really obvious when dealing with the simplicity that is necessary for character drawing. Even Pathfinder does not work very well in this environment (though I miss it).

You will need to change your working style as you become accustomed to the Fontographer paradigm. WARN-ING! It is quite possible that you will become addicted to Fontographer's tools. Of course, this is heresy of the worst kind. I expect to be castigated severely and realize that my life is hanging by a thread. But we really must deal with reality. Freehand, Fontographer, & FontLab all have far superior shape drawing tools. In fact, now that I have Fontographer again, I can hardly stand drawing in Illustrator.

The Key is in the keypad

Fontographer takes me back to when I could draw—changing tools as necessary with the numerical keypad. All of the basic drawing functions are accessed with 0-9. Editing is all done with the Selection tool (which can be accessed with the Command key or the Grave) and a small group of keyboard shortcuts. It all becomes habitual very quickly and the software recedes into the background allowing me to focus on the actual drawing of the characters.

The sinister benefit

I think that part of my enthusiasm for this drawing process is that it works extremely well for left-handed people who run the mouse with their left hand and the numerical keypad with the right hand. Because that scenario is very rare, it's a real joy to have an application fit my hands like that. [Of course, artists and graphic designers have a much higher percentage of left-handed people than the world population in general.]

Here are some essential editing shortcuts

❦ Retract BCPs (Handles): [Command+R] This shortcut [and the three Convert Point shortcuts] take the place of the Convert Point portion of AI's Pen tool. To make a sharp corner point out of a point with handles, select the point(s), hit the shortcut and the handles retract to zero length.

❦ Clean up paths: [Command+Shift+C] This command simplifies paths and most importantly adds points to the *extrema*. Having points on the extrema is essential to font design.

 Extrema for PostScript paths: These are those locations on a curve that are at the extreme left, right, top, or bottom. To reword, those places where a vertical line would touch the left or right edges of a curve in a tangent, or the places where a horizontal line would touch the top or bottom edges of a curve in a tangent. PostScript Type 1 fonts require this, but all font paths work much better if you have points on all the extrema.

Other path problems to fix

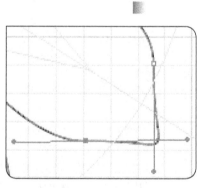

❦ Crossing handles: This also solves the problem with crossing handles (like those seen to the right). These are an absolute no-no—bad design, faulty paths, ugly shapes, and so on. The resultant kinks which are produced in the curves require more points to make them work within a font.

 You need to get in the habit of cleaning up the paths regularly: I usually uncheck Simplify because it modifies my paths. If you use it, I recommend setting the simplify slider at the minimum [1]. Even then you will deal a bit with path modifications, but it is far preferable to the other option—paths which cause you problems. As mentioned, it is always good to add extrema.

❦ Too many points: At the right of the capture below
are the paths of a lowercase a in a font called
Blackmoor LET that I found on my computer. As
you can see the right-hand set of paths have a
ridiculous number of points. It appears to be an
auto-trace of some kind. More than that, all the
right-hand points are corner points. There is not a
single curve point in those paths. You can set up
your auto-trace options to do that. On the left is
a quick conversion to a more reasonable amount
of points. The points were deleted by marqueeing
them with the selection tool and then merged
(using that essential shortcut already mentioned,
Merge Point [Command+M]).

I'll admit it needs to be tweaked to match the
roughness of the original. It needs to be cleaned
up, also. But the paths are much more usable,
editable, and will almost certainly print better.
Even if you decide you need to leave the shapes
as all corner points, about half of the points
can be eliminated without changing the shapes
noticeably. Look at the three side by side points
at the bottom of the counter, for example. All
three of them can probably be deleted.

❦ Points on top of each other: In addition, fonts can not have points on top of each other. This most commonly occurs when designers who do not know how to use the Pen tool or do not know how to produce usable shapes, try to make a finished shape by drawing separate closed paths and then try to combine them into a single closed path with the remove overlap command.

 Adjust preferences: Fontographer will show you points on top of each other with a little dashed circle around the points.

The good news is that cleaning up paths will fix most of these problems. The other good news is that end points dropped on top of each other are automatically merged. You'll probably need to modify your drawing style to include more open paths. If you have a lot of Illustrator or FontLab experience, this will take a little adjustment.

❦ Correct Path Direction: [Command+Shift+K] This command is needed because composite paths in fonts are produced by reversing the path direction. This produces what is called even/odd fill. For some reason, Adobe has a real tough time with this concept. Altsys never did. Path directions are usually what you expect. If they are not, then this command will fix it. (You can see such problems in the preview [Command+L] and in the font window.) Using this command will make interior paths knock out of the enclosing path—producing the opening (counter) in the bowl of the b and d, for example.

❦ Remove overlap: [Command+Shift+O] This combines two overlapping paths like the Unite command in Pathfinder. It also fixes paths that loop around on themselves. If the path directions are not correct, the portions that overlap are left inside the united path, but all you need to do is double-click on the interior pieces and hit the Delete key to get rid of them.

Type Command+Shift+K first: I have gotten in the habit correcting the path direction first, before I use the Remove Overlap command. It just saves time by eliminating all the times I have to undo or double-click the interior shape remainders to delete them.

The convert point commands

- ❦ Curve Point: [Command+8]

- ❦ Corner point: [Command+9]

- ❦ Tangent Point: [Command+0]

> **Tip: Fit in Window**
>
> Because Command+Zero is used by the Tangent Point command, "Fit in Window" is Command+T instead of the Adobe norm of Command+Zero.

One things Adobe Pen tool users will need to change is their reliance on the convert point tool. Fontographer uses three convert point commands that work much more effectively. If I want to move the handles individually on a curve point, for example, all I do is type Command+9 to convert it to a corner point. Then the handles move independently.

Conversely, if I have two handles pulled out of a corner point, I can quickly lock them into a common tangent and auto-curve the path at that point by selecting the point and then typing Command+8 to convert the corner point to a curve point. Then I can easily edit the handles with the Selection tool.

It works the same way if I need to move the handle of a tangent point to the side. Simply type the command to convert the tangent point to either a curve or corner point and drag the handle where it needs to be.

The Pen Tool

 The Pen tool is the core of PostScript illustration: It was invented by Fontographer. This is the exact same tool FreeHand had until Macromedia caved in to the AI standard. It is much more simple than the four-part tool Illustrator, Photoshop, and InDesign use for drawing paths. What I need to say is simple: "You must become fluent with the Pen tool!" This is not an option.

As mentioned, you simply click to produce a corner point, and click-drag to produce a curve point. I'll review path construction in a bit.

How do you add that Pen tool skill?

If you have not used it before, this is a very strange tool that does not seem intuitive at all. There is nothing like it anywhere else except in PostScript drawing programs. Even if you are very familiar with Adobe programs, you may have never learned to use the Pen tool well.

So let's talk a little about how you gain skill. I found this out when I went to the University of Minnesota in the late '60s to learn to be a fine artist. When I went to the orientation session of my first drawing class, the final thing the professor said as we left (planning on coming back on Monday morning to have him "teach" us to draw) was, "Oh, by the way — when you come Monday, bring sixty drawings that you have done over the weekend. I don't care what you draw, but you must bring sixty new drawings done in the next three days."

During that first nine-week course, we all drew nearly 600 drawings each in pencil, conté crayon, charcoal, crowquill, and heavy bamboo dip pen. The first ones were horrible and I threw them away. I wish I had them now. I didn't produce my first "keepers" until my second year, after four drawing courses, two painting courses, three courses on color theory, and so forth. By that time I had produced thousands of drawings, hundreds of stupid exercises, and more than twenty large paintings. They were starting to get fairly good — surprise, surprise!

You will have to do the same thing with the Pen tool. You just need to draw. As we get into drawing fonts, you need to draw letter shapes. Your real assignment, for the next few months, is to draw at least two dozen characters a week with the Pen tool. Do not assemble them from pieces. Draw them in their entirety— one closed path at a time. In reality, I hope you will do many more than that. By the time you finish, you will be getting pretty good with the Pen tool.

So, how does the Pen tool work?

So, with that intro, how does the tool work? When you simply click with the Pen, you produce corner points having no handles. The cap T at the left could be produced this way. If you hold down the Shift key while clicking, the new point location will be constrained to horizontal, vertical, or 45° angles from the previous point.

When you click and then immediately drag, while still holding down the button, a curve point is produced. You drag out the outgoing handle which produces an equal incoming handle on the other side of the point on the same tangent as the handle you are dragging out. With these two options you can draw anything your little heart desires — easy, huh? That's how the R was drawn.

Actually it is that easy. You can modify any point as you draw by holding down the command key to get the Selection tool. The click on the point to move it and/or edit the handles. Just click on the end point before you release the selection tool to continue drawing the line. Once you become accustomed to the tool, you will be amazed with its precision, dazzled by its fluidity, and addicted to its editable flexibility.

Constraining the tool: When clicking to produce corner points, holding down the Shift key will keep the points lined up on horizontal, vertical, or 45° angles. When click-dragging to produce a curve point, holding down the Shift key will cause the handles to be on horizontal, vertical, or 45° angles.

Constraining vertically or horizontally are very handy when placing points at the extrema.

As you are drawing, if you do not like the way the handles are arranged, or the shape of a segment, simply press down the Command key to access the Selection tool. Click on a point or the handles to adjust the point location and the handle angles. If you add the Option Key, you can Option-drag on the endpoint to drag out the handle from that corner point. Then release the Command key to go back to the Pen tool. If necessary, click on the end point to select it before releasing the Command key. Then you can continue to draw the path.

 VERY IMPORTANT TIP: Every shape should be drawn in one continuous path with points at all the extrema. This is the most common mistake of beginning pen tool users. If you have trouble with the extrema, type the shortcut [Command+Shift+C] to clean up the paths. You can do this regularly as you go, if needed. **IN FACT:** as much as possible, you should merge all points by hand that are not extrema.

Deleting and merging points

If you select a point or points and delete it or them, the path will be broken, and become an open path. If you select a point or points and merge it or them [Command+M], the point or points will disappear and the segment will be auto-curved. Merging points is a good way to smooth out curves. Clean Up Paths to add the extrema as needed.

Joining and closing paths

All paths in a font must be closed. Fontographer deals with this better than any app I have used. You simply drop any end point on top of another end point and they automatically merge into a single point—closing the path. Normally, you will immediately type Command+M to merge that new point out of existence.

Joining open paths could not be easier. The same way a path is automatically closed, two paths become one by simply moving an endpoint of one path on top of an endpoint of another.

Composite paths

A composite path is used in Postscript illustration apps (Illustrator and InDesign) to make an interior path knock out of an exterior path. This produces an open empty hole in the shape. The most common place we see these composite paths are in letters like BDOPQabdegopq. We cannot place a white shape on top of the black shapes. The letters would look correct on a black background but produce white spots all over a colored background.

In most applications (especially Adobe apps) you need to be careful of your composite paths: You spend a lot of time messing with them because Adobe has never gotten composite paths down very well. On the other hand, Altsys has never really had any problems at all with composite paths. FreeHand always called it even/odd fill. But the bottomline is that there has never been any real issues with composite paths in any Altsys developed application.

In my FontLab book, I had to spend quite a bit of time talking about path direction. Path direction is what determines whether a path will punch a hole in the path it overlaps. For Fontographer I will probably not mention this issue much. All you need to do is type the shortcut for Correct Path Direction [Command+Shift+K]. In my experience, this always solves the problem.

Fixing the font direction of the entire font

In fact, my normal procedure is to regularly (when I am in the Font Window) Select All [Command+A] and then correct the path direction [Command+Shift+K] for the entire font. I do not do it as often as I do the Save command, but I use it several times while I am designing a font and every time I see any filling problems in the font window.

*Composite paths are simply
no problem in Fontographer*

Your assignment for now

Draw! You need to draw character shapes. Draw in Fontographer—draw & draw & draw.

Now it's time to begin

I wouldn't dream of proposing a standard design procedure

I am going to design a few fonts and let you watch. There is no standard method for creating fonts. All I am trying to do here is give you various scenarios that you can adapt to your needs while designing fonts. Please let me know if you see anything missing, or if you want me to add something else I don't mention. Again, all I am going to do is design a font with multitudinous comments hoping to cover most of the bases.

A revised decorative font

Why do I want to start with a modified font? I realize that most of you do not have a ready library of fonts you have already designed. My intention is to put some free fonts on a page at Hackberry for you to play with.

A feel for the process

I want to start here to give you a feel for the process and teach you some of the basic things you'll need to know when we go on to the design of a font family. Unless you know some of these basics, any discussion of font design will be very choppy.

To the left you see Cutlass. I've always liked this font, but I really want another one that is more narrow and a lot lighter. So my goal is a font that is usable in text or display, picking up the general look of Cutlass and converting it to a headline font with grace and style. That's a stretch for my abilities, but that's my goal.

Cutlass

ABCDEFGHIJ
KLMNOPQR
STUVWXYZ
1234567890

abcdefghijk
lmnopqrst
uvwxyz

I designed this one while I was writing one of the FontLab versions of Practical Font Design. It was based on a scan scrap I saw in Typophile.

I thought I'd show you a copy of the scan to show where this font began for me. Every font is different. You never know from where your inspiration will come.

Of course, the other part of this is the simple fact that if I gave you a project where we all developed a font from the same scan, they would all be quite different. But this was the source for Cutlass. You can find a copy of this font on the Fontographer page of the Hackberry Font Foundry (hackberry-fonts.com). It is called Decorative.fog. Download it and open it in Fontographer.

Picking a name

Before we start designing, I need a working name. Fontographer does not play well unless you name the font and fill in the other parameters in the Font Info dialog box. We will have to make some basic assumptions right now as we get started about ascender, cap height, x-height, and descender, plus overshoots. Many of these will probably change as we go through the process, but it needs to be started before you begin. Let's go through them quickly.

The Font Info dialog

The command to open this is found under the Element menu [Shortcut: Command+Option+F]. Let's take a look at the various pages. Click on Advanced.

Names

I decided on Poniard because it is a slender dagger from the Renaissance. This font is like Cutlass (the source of Decorative.fog) but small and slender, so I made a decision. I made the weight Regular (that is, it does not show

with the font name). I used all the Design Parameters with
the choices in parentheses because I do not want them used
as part of the full name. As you can see, I had to uncheck
building names automatically so I could delete the word
Regular from the name manually. This should work fine.

Dimensions

The best definition for UPM is Units Per eM. It probably stands for something more esoteric. Regardless, it sets
the number of divisions in your em (the height of your font).
PostScript fonts use 1000. It is an easy figure to deal with.
For some reason TrueType fonts use 2048 for their UPM. I
would always change the em to 1000 and let Fontographer
scale them. If for no other reason than it is easier to adjust
vertical dimension percentages in my head using 1000.

Key Dimensions

The UPM is what contains your characters. Here you
have to make some more decisions. This is where you set
the vertical measurements of the font: ascender, cap height,
x-height, and descender. Yes, you can modify them later,

but it is a hassle. So what shall we use for Poniard? This is where the font design begins.

As usual, my tastes have changed since I drew Cutlass in 2010. This is normal. My typographic tastes are constantly changing. What I need to do at this point is develop a sense of style for Poniard. I'm coming at this cold for your edification so I can give you a feel for what you go through in making these decisions.

Font Information		

Mode: ○ Easy ● Advanced

| Names | Dimensions | Encoding | Credits | Licensing | Recommendations |

UPM size (em square): 1000 ▾ ○ Retain path coordinates when changing UPM size
● Scale all glyphs according to UPM size change

☐ Calculate all values at: 113.7% ▾ (Calc All)

Family linespacing
Should be identical in all fonts within the family
Typographic linespacing values:

Ascender:	700	(Calc)
Descender:	-300	(Calc)
Line gap:	0	(Calc)

Safe zone (Windows GDI clipping zone):

Safe zone top:	697	(Calc)
Safe zone bottom:	-303	(Calc)

Individual font dimensions
Should reflect actual dimensions of each individual font
Typographic dimensions:

Caps height:	650	(Calc)
x height:	300	(Calc)
Italic angle:	0	

Underline (only some applications use this):

Underline position:	-100	(Calc)
Underline width:	50	

Line Gap:
This seems to be some PC thing and the manual says to set it at Zero unless you have a compelling reason. So I did.

ncel) (OK)

This particular demo is arbitrary, so it should be quite bit of fun. What I have been looking for over the past few months is a "swashy" yet a bit prickly decorative font to use for headlines. I want it to be slender, elegant, reeking with style—whatever that all means.

When I opened Cutlass, I found the following dimensions. I was surprised at all the things that were changed by FontLab upon Saving.

Evidently FontLab radically changes things when you save the font. The Dimensions in FontLab are:

- ❦ Ascender: 745
- ❦ Cap Height: 670
- ❦ X-Height: 480
- ❦ Descender: -205

Upon converting to Fontographer, Cutlass is set at:

- ❦ Ascender: 718
- ❦ Cap Height: 670
- ❦ X-Height: 480
- ❦ Descender: -340

Typographic linespacing values:			Typographic dimensions:		
Ascender:	718	Calc	Caps height:	670	Calc
Descender:	-340	Calc	x height:	480	Calc
Line gap:	79	Calc	Italic angle:	0	
Safe zone (Windows GDI clipping zone):			Underline (only some applications use this):		
Safe zone top:	753	Calc	Underline position:	-100	Calc
Safe zone bottom:	-340	Calc	Underline width:	50	

None of this really matters, but it certainly explains some of the screwy things I've seen for measurements when I open a font to take a look and see how they designed the font. What I need to do now is come up with some measurements that make sense for Poniard. So I look at the font on the screen as try to figure out what I need to do to make it fit my vision.

First, some practical stuff about measurements

As you probably know from setting type, an em is defined as a square which is the point size of the type. In a font this is measured from the top of the ascender to the bottom of the descender. We always want this total to match my UPM.

If it does not match you can have some severe problems. I think I can assume you've been forced to mess with
Zapfino. As you know, the characters in that Mac system font
are colossal. To see what is causing this, I opened Zapfino in
both FontLab and Fontographer. Fontographer made some
radical changes to the settings.

There really is a major problem with this font. In Font-
Lab the UPM is set at 1000, but the dimensions are immense.

- Ascender: 1692
- Cap Height: 1110
- X-Height: 550
- Descender: -1285

No wonder it's torture to try to set type with this
font. In addition, Zapf didn't even bother to stay within the
ridiculous dimensions set. What further surprised me was
the changes seen when I opened Zapfino in Fontographer.
Remember, this doesn't matter except for the fact that we
need to set up something rational for our own use.

First of all the UPM was changed to 400. Why? I have
no idea. The dimensions seem to be simply scaled, but they
are still absurd.

- Ascender: 677
- Cap Height: 444
- X-Height: 220
- Descender: -514

Welcome to the wild and wacky world of font design.

The good news is that we really do not have to worry
about these things. Let the industry confuse itself. What we
need to do is come up with a rational set up for our font
designs that will meet our needs. You need to get it under
control in your own mind. All you need to do is pick dimen-

sions which fall into the "normal range"—which is quite wide. So, let's talk a little historically here—recent history.

Some ballpark dimension standards

All design parameters in font design are out of control. There really is no standard—rather, everyone has their own standards. For centuries people have been doing whatever they felt like and letting the various fonts fall where they may on these things. The problem for us, as font designers, is to make sense of things and fit our font designs within this mess in such a way that the users of the font recognize what has been done and are able to fit its design into a historical setting in their mind that makes sense.

Be careful of seeking advice

Like all things typographic, I am certain that you could go to typophile.com and pose a question that would erupt into a massive debate and teach you little. Everyone would have their own firmly held and stanchly defended opinion. Remember, as a general rule, the more rabid the defensive position the more insecure the opinion holder really is. You need to make your own decisions.

All of that being said, you are responsible to educate yourself and come to a personal, well-reasoned position with which you are comfortable. Typophile, mentioned above, is an excellent resource. The subconscious reaction we are seeking from ourself and the users of our font is, *"That works!"* Of course, you know that phrase is subjective nonsense. But that is what we are dealing with—our own subjective sense of right and wrong. Let's talk about some basic norms.

The phototype norm from the 1970s & '80s

Companies like Compugraphic who produced phototype equipment in the 1970s and '80s had very rigid standards. It was taught to me as follows: x-height one third, ascender one third, and descender one third. All the film strips we purchased in the 1980s fit this arbitrary rigid standard. This was coupled with another: the cap height is 4%

less than the ascender. So this group of type designs would give us the following normal settings:

- ❦ Ascender: 667
- ❦ Cap Height: 640
- ❦ X-Height: 333
- ❦ Descender: −333

Now, rest assured, these dimensions do not fit anything I have seen since I started designing fonts in the 1990s. In fact, though I have not studied this, I have never seen a font with these dimensions except for old Compugraphic film strips. All of those fonts had these dimensions. It looked normal to those of us trained during that period. And now, for this book, it does give our mind a rack to hang our hat upon.

So, how does all of this affect me as I make my decisions for Poniard? It just goes into my personal creative data processing within my head. All of this is built upon experience. What you need to do is open up fonts that you like and see what their dimensions are. You will find things widely vary—seemingly at random. But as you look fonts over, you will come to some conclusions about what you like personally. That is an essential part of font design. In many ways, this is fine art. And I remember my professors hammering on me the following dictum as rigid doctrine.

As an artist, good is defined as what you like and bad is defined as what you don't like

That is certainly the case in font design. The problem, of course, is defining what you like and don't like. This takes concentrated effort over years of practice. Assuming that you are an experienced graphic designer, you have almost certainly developed a sense of style and taste.

But you are just starting out as a font designer. This is why you need to go through your font collection and open all the fonts you like and see what they did for dimensions.

More than that you need to look at fonts you like which have the feel you want for your new font.

To review: Decorative uses this

- ☙ Ascender: 718
- ☙ Cap Height: 670
- ☙ X-Height: 480
- ☙ Descender: −340

I want to fit things within the 1000 UPM. I want the x-height quite a bit shorter. Decorative.fog now seems so eightyish—whatever that means. My tastes have changed over the past year. So, I make some decisions. As mentioned, they are simply arbitrary, but based on my experience. Your values will differ and it will change the look of your font.

My decision is to set the metrics for Poniard like this:

- ☙ Ascender: 700
- ☙ Cap Height: 650
- ☙ X-Height: 300
- ☙ Descender: −300

At this point, I click OK and set myself the task of setting guides for this new font that will work within my new settings. Here again, things are not what they seem, so let me take you through that process. (At this point, I have done a Save As to the revised Decorative font file, changing the name to Poniard.fog, in its own new folder.)

Using the Layers palette

Fontographer has done a good thing here. If I open a character window, I will see to the lower left a little palette called layers. It has four choices:

- ☙ Outline: this is where the paths for the font are located. This is where I draw my font.

- ☙ Template: This is where I place scans of characters I have drawn for tracing. If the font was originally designed in FontLab and you are converting it from that .vfb file, you may find the paths from the font used as a mask there. It is also a good place to draw pieces without interacting with the Outline layer. You can simply Cut and Paste them into the outline layer as needed.

* Guides: here you can drag out or hand draw guides to help you size your characters and keep them consistent. The guides on this layer are all global— that is, they appear in every Outline window

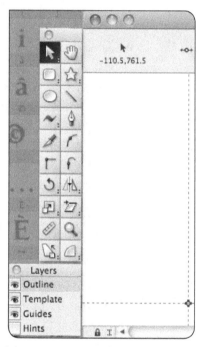

* Hints: Let's start with the user manual here. "Use the Hints layer to specify how smaller sizes of a glyph will be printed when output to the screen or low-resolution printers." Now – I might get shot for saying this – but I confess that I never check this box and that I don't really care about hints. So far, that attitude hasn't hurt me in any way of which I am aware. I don't design fonts with screen display in mind and I haven't used a low resolution printer since some time in the early 1990s. I work with Macs and hinting plays little or no part in what I see as I work. That being said, there are experienced and successful type designers who take special care to hint their fonts. They test and manually tweak the results. But as with drawing outlines, there is no surefire formula that I can sum up for you in a book. All I can do is present the facts and give you the foundation for the further development of your skills.

There are two types of hinting: Postscript (or Type 1) hinting, and TrueType hinting. Fontographer 5 will only display PostScript (Type 1) hints, not TrueType hints. However, be aware that there is an important connection between the two kinds of hints: Fontographer uses the PS hints as a guide when auto-generating TrueType hints when you output a TTF file. So, inexact or inappropriate PS hints can mean really bad looking TrueType fonts if TrueType is what you're trying to output. There is no way to predict the result, either. You have to take a look at the TrueType font in an environment that interprets TT hints, like Windows.

Hinting is the voodoo of font design. There are cases where no hinting turns out to be the best choice. Here's veteran type designer Mark Simonson on the subject:

> "There are some cases where hints do not help, such as with irregular font designs and with complex font designs (e.g., outlined styles). Very bold styles will also confuse the autohinter. I find that these usually need to be done manually. Hints are of limited use for slanted faces, but I find that setting alignment zones ("blues") is very important."

Should you have the need, getting the hang of PS hinting isn't all that difficult as compared to TT hinting. It's simply a matter of taking the time to hint and compare, hint and compare, and you will acquire the knack. Here's Mark Simonson again:

> "My test regimen is fairly informal. I take a look at the font in InDesign and other Adobe apps and make print-outs on a 600 dpi laser printer. The main things I look for are uneven text color (sometimes this is more of a design issue), inconsistent alignment on the baseline, x-height, and cap height, distorted character shapes, inconsistent stroke thickness, parts of letters filling in where they shouldn't. I also test on Windows XP using simple apps that come with it. Adobe apps will perform nearly identically from Mac to Windows, so I don't test those on Windows."

Web Fonts: Today, the TrueType format is, by far, the most widely supported format for the web. There is really only one reason for this: TrueType is the most all-purpose format. The Microsoft web browser rendering engines - Windows GDI and the new DirectWrite engine - are geared to give the best onscreen results with hinted TrueType fonts. Plus, in any version of Internet Explorer less than IE9 or on any version of IE on Windows XP, there is no option but TrueType. And this is not just an IE-only thing: it affects any browser running on Windows - Firefox, Chrome, and Opera, too. There are about a billion Windows users in the world.

On the Apple side, TrueType fonts automatically adjust gracefully on the Mac with visual results nearly indistinguishable (and perhaps superior) to what you would see with an OTF font. The Apple rasterizers simply ignore the hints inside the font and interpret the outlines much as they would the PS outlines in an OTF font. The Mac, in effect, "hints on the fly" basing its decisions only on the outlines and font metrics. This is what happens on all Apple devices, including iOS devices like iPhone and iPad.

As a result of this, Apple users rarely see a need to worry about all of this stuff, and they'll probably buy your fonts without foreseeing any problems. However, unless you are certain that your niche is exclusively Mac users, you will do well to consider all the customers who will need hinted fonts to be able to comfortably read normal body copy. Again, there are a roughly a billion users of Windows.

My Final Advice: I recommend that you read the manual for an explanation of the three selections in Fontographer's Hinting menu. Understand the difference between manual and automatic PS hinting. It's also a good idea to experiment at least a little and output a few TTF fonts to see what happens. But between me and thee, I wouldn't even know what to look for. For me, the hinting of PostScript outlines, the converting of those Postscript outlines to TrueType outlines, and then the working out of the TrueType hints, adds up to a massive level of complication and tedium which detracts from my focus on simply creating good-looking fonts which work well for my books. It also detracts from the fun of doing it! Once I have a solid set of well-drawn outlines, everything else flows from that. And I can worry about hinting later if and when I have to. I therefore regard hinting as a series of post-design steps that I'd much rather leave to someone else who specializes, and continue to focus on the job at hand.

On a positive note, there is no question that once high-pixel density screens like the iPhone retina are ubiquitous, hinting will be unnecessary. It could be many years, but the day will come—probably sooner than we expect.

Setting guides

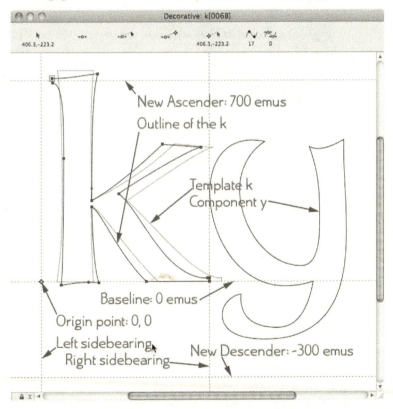

For now what we want to do is add guides to show us where our dimensions are. As you can see in the capture above, Fontographer has added guidelines at the ascender and descender.

The problem is that the character window is really featureless as you begin. There is no visible grid or ruler. I feel lost when I look at it. What I want is a way to locate my character shapes that will give me control and consistency. To have any hope of keeping all of this together, I really need to add many more guides. Here's where we are starting. I used the k character and added a y because it shows both an ascender and a descender.

Guides are added by dragging them out of the Origin or Baseline guides given to us by Fontographer. Because there is no ruler this can be a little tricky. You need to use the Info Bar at the top of the outline window. As you drag up a new guide, the numbers change. Here's the numbers for the new cap height guide.

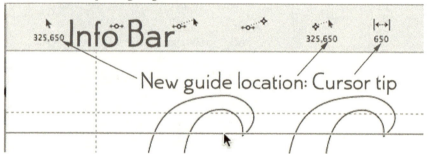

When I release the mouse, a new guideline appears at 650 em units, which is where I set my cap height.

I need guides for the following:

- ❦ Cap Height

- ❦ X-height

- ❦ All the overshoots: I'll need overshoots for the cap height, x-height, and baseline. The overshoots for the ascender and descender are usually helpful, but I need to make them inside the UPM size. So they go below the ascender and above the descender (if you decide to use them).

Remember about the overshoots?

Originally, I had a graphic about type terminology very early in the book that showed the Optical Alignment areas or overshoots. It seems better to get right into font design so that was moved.. We are talking about optical alignment—fixing it so our brain sees things as aligned. To do that you need to run curves and points beyond the baseline, x-height and cap height dimensions. I have found that 15 emus works well for me. You may want to change that.

I only add an overshoot for the cap height, x-height, and baseline. I used to add them to the ascender and descender, but it caused font sizing problems. So, I quit doing that. The guidelines I need for the overshoots in this case are: Cap Height: 665; X-height: 315; & Baseline: -15. If I were going to add the Ascender/descender guides they would be at 685 and -285.

It looks like this for the period character when I get all the guides added. Remember, add it in one character and they show up in all of them. Guides are always movable in the guides layer and you delete a guide by dragging it back into the baseline origin

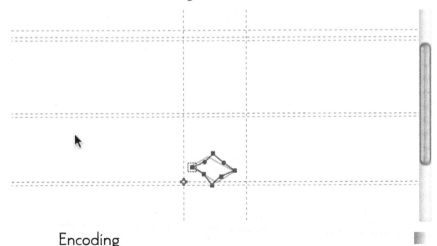

Encoding

For now, let's just leave this alone. This can of worms will be dealt with as we go through the process—both for

Poniard and for the font family that follows. The main thing
is that this controls the number of character slots. Decora-
tive.fog has 260.

Credits

Here you fill in your own information. It will vary a lot.
For example, I never put anything in under vendor. I have
several vendors who sell my fonts. The way Fontographer
works, they think the vendor has the copyright. This is not
true in my case—and probably not in your case either. So for
vendor I use the name of my foundry and its URL.

Designer

Yes, this is you. You do want to let people know who owns the rights to the design. A URL to an online bio is a good idea.

Copyright

You own the copyright (unless you have signed a contract giving someone else the rights).

Creation date

I always click the now button when I fill out this page. For me this is when the font design becomes real. You do it the way that makes sense to you.

Licensing

License Information

Again, over-protective paranoia does not serve you well here. But that is your decision to make. The five copy license has become the new standard. As you can see, I make a simple statement. The big thing is to deal with a major personal decision.

Are you going to spend a lot of time protecting your rights (& paying lawyers), or would you rather be designing?

That is your decision to make.

But remember licenses are like warranties. The more complex and restrictive they are the more users look for loopholes and try to circumvent the legalities. Personally, I let the Lord cover it—He's more than able.

Recommendations

You can make these recommendations, but no one will ever see them. So, I am not sure why they are offered. No software I know of gives you access to this information except Fontographer.

Setting up your workspace

For those of you that are former students of mine, you know how much I harp on setting up your applications to fit your working style. Preferences, shortcuts, and toolbars need to be controlled. Careful attention needs to be paid as you work to notice repetitive tasks that you can do with a shortcut or where you can place the toolbar or dialog box within easy reach. As you get them set up you will find yourself working two to three times as fast.

Limited control in Fontographer

The only problem with that is that Fontographer preference choices are very limited. There are no toolbars. You cannot customize shortcuts. The only thing you can do is set up your toolbar and layers palette where they are comfortable. The rest of the preferences are really personal and you can check them out in just a couple minutes. I find that the defaults are pretty good, and Fontographer is very efficient.

Dealing with shortcuts,

As usual, you memorize the ones you use regularly. At this point, I am editing the book after designing the first seven fonts mentioned in this book. As I have become reacquainted with Fontographer (and it has been great fun) I have quite naturally picked up the shortcuts for most of the commands listed under the Element and Point menus. They are the only ones I use regularly enough to memorize.

But at this point, there is only one thing to do.

It's time to get to work!

Modifying a font

We have the font named, saved, and ready to modify. So, where do we start? Wherever it makes sense to you. For this modification I'm going to start by fixing the lowercase.

I want to start there for several reasons. The primary one is that I have made the x-height so much smaller. I might as well deal with that right from the beginning. That choice is really going to dominate the look of the new style. What's going to happen is that the lowercase characters are not going to be condensed even though the caps will be. The caps, ascenders, and descenders are going to be elongated.

What I was going to do was scale horizontally about 65%. Then I calculated how much I changed the x-height. That turned out to be nearly 65% also.

So, this has turned out to be a very simple one step transformation. As you can see below, I can apply up to four at once. I selected the lowercase a-z character slots in the Font window [with a click-drag] . Then I opened the Transform dialog [using the shortcut: Command+\]. I set the first transformation to scale uniformly at 65% and hit the Return key to execute the Transform command.

Transform

Transformation Center: ◆ Basepoint

Transformations:

Choose up to four consecutive transformations to perform with the selection.

First: 🔲 Scale Uniformly | 65 |

Second: Do Nothing

Third: Do Nothing

Fourth: Do Nothing

Cancel   Transform

It was very clean and quick. At first glance, it looks like the scaling was perfect—cleaner than FontLab. But then it may just be Fontographer's clean interface.

I'm going to start with the b

I double-click it to open the character window. This is the first look my mind has with the reality of the design I have been thinking about for several days. But it's like they always say about a battle...

All plans disappear at the first click of the mouse.

Now you have to begin the process of getting a feel for what you are going to do and what the font is going to look like. So, let's get started.

1. Marquee the stem top: Click and drag it up to the new ascender height while holding down the shift key.

2. Marquee the notch point plus the four points that make up the shoulder: Move them down with the arrow keys until the top of the bowl aligns with the x-height overshoot.

 Arrow key editing: The arrow keys move a selection by 10 emus. Add the Shift key and it moves 100 emus. Use the Option key and it moves 1 emu. You can change the 10 emu preference.

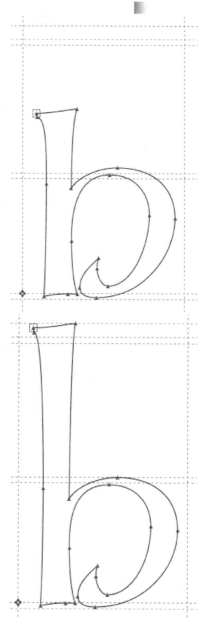

3. I like the look but the stem looks a bit heavy: Using the measurement tool, I find that the stem is 70 emus wide and the widest part of the bowl is 69 emus. So at least part of the bulk is an illusion. But what it looks like I am dealing with here is that I measured the narrowest part of the stem and widest part of the bowl.

4. So, I marquee the right side of the stem and the bowl: I hold down the Option key and move the selection sideways. At 4 emus it looks good to me.

5. The huge flare at the top of the stem is next: I select the top handle of the point at the center of the left side of the stem and drag it way up toward the top. (I had to hit Command+8 to convert the tangent point to a curve point before it would let me do it.)

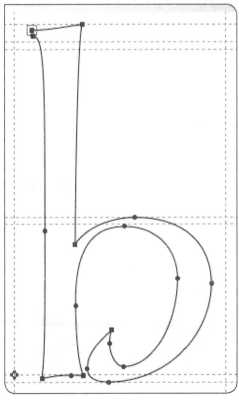

6. Fixed the bottom flare: Same way.

7. I grabbed the tail of the bowl: I moved it down to the overshoot and sideways to the right 2 emus.

8. It's done! I like it.

9. Well, not quite.

Building a pieces glyph

As I look at the b I see that the stroke minimums are very different from the upper left to the lower right of the bowl. I also notice in the font window that the curve where the shoulder comes off the stem is so thin that is disappears. I decide to fix that. What I need are a good set of weight balls. This is something I do early on in every font design.

What are weight balls?

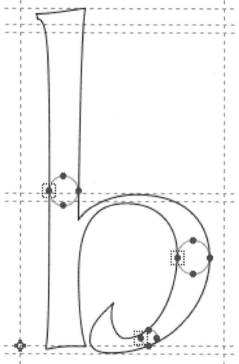

Weight balls are a device I use (learned from Leslie Cabarga's "Bible") which enable me to measure stroke widths (and other things as needed) to keep them consistent. I draw them on the Template layer. The reason I use the template layer is that I want these shapes to be separated from the outline of the character. This makes them easier to cut and store in a special character slot.

I draw them with the Oval tool holding down the Shift and Option keys so I can draw from the center out. I draw three balls at this time. One at the narrowest part of the tail of the bowl. This is my minimum width. One at the widest part of the bowl. This is my maximum width. Plus, a final one at the narrowest part of the stem. The stem width is usually a little more narrow than the maximum. But that depends on the axis. If you are designing a font with a rational axis (vertical), then the maximum and stem widths are the same.

Because they are on the template layer all I need to do is use Select All [Command+A] and Cut [Command+X]. Now that they are on the clipboard I need a place to put them. For that, I'll need a blank, unused character slot. I'll need to make one.

Generating a new character slot

Generating a new glyph slot in a Fontographer font is a little tricky but not too bad. What I need to do is go to the encoding page of font info and add one character to the number I find there. Then I got to the Font window and select the new slot generated. I type the shortcut for Selection Info [Command+I] And I get this dialog.

Glyph Information

Glyph Name:	ll|	Get From: (Unicode) (Encoding)
Unicode Codepoint:		Get From: (Name)
Unicode Name:		

▶ Contour and fill properties (Type 3 fonts)

(Cancel) (OK)

I type in ll and click OK. Originally, I used Alef (the first Hebrew letter) and then clicked the Name button next to Unicode Codepoint. This got me a symbol in the character slot. However, this one character made my font list with the Hebrew fonts in the InDesign font list. So, I went back to ll (which is what I use in FontLab). If you do not like that, use whatever you like. Mainly, you need a new slot at the end of all the slots you are using for the font so you can have easy access to select it to use the pieces—as you'll see in a little bit.

Setting up the pieces glyph

I open the ll slot (labeled **), select the Outline layer and paste in the newly drawn weight balls. I move them around to arrange them for easy use. I also add an outlined square surrounding the three balls. I quickly found that the component of the weight balls has a wide grey line around it that was covering up the edges of the weight balls when the component was selected. You see what I mean next as we fix the weight of the b character.

Fixing the weight of the b character

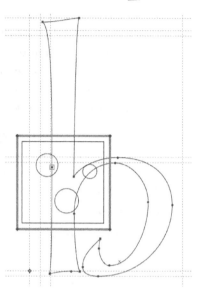

I return to the font window, and select the ll slot. It'll be the last one and have a ** name in the Font Window. I use the Copy Component command under the Edit menu [Command+G]. Then I open the b slot and paste in the component. I can immediately see that the stroke width for the upper left of the bowl is far too small.

Please notice the dark grey line round the component. You can see that if I had not made the box, it would block the edge of the balls. (The double square is optional, but it allows me to see what I have in the ll slot in the Font window. These pieces glyphs get very complex, as I'll show you later.)

Using the pieces component

I can easily select the path under the component and adjust it to the proper width. To check the various widths throughout the glyph I simply click on the component and move it around.

 Be careful not to accidently resize: If you grab the corner of a component, you can resize it. If that happens just Undo [Command+Z]. It is critical that the balls remain the correct size.

I move the interior point at the top of the bowl to the right and down. The I adjust the left handle of that point and the top handle of the other point on the segment controlling the other end. I adjust it approximately into position.

Then I merge that top point [Command+M] of the shoulder and Clean Up Paths [Command+Shift+C] with the simplify option unchecked. This auto-curves the line beautifully and adds a point back to the extrema without messing up the curve.

I quickly check the other widths, and delete the component. Now the b is done. I also have the start of my pieces glyph. I will be gradually be adding pieces to use for glyph assembly as we go through the font design process.

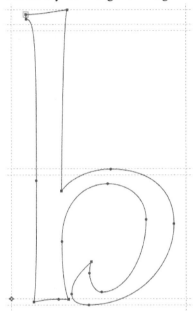

Fixing the p

I open the p character and immediately paste in the pieces component. It was easy to see here that I had some real issues. The first thing I notice is that in the p the tail of the bowl is much lighter and thinner.

Adding pieces to the pieces slot

I decide to cut a tail off the b and place it into the pieces slot (the ll). I go back to the b. I choose the Knife tool by typing a 7. I use it to cut off the tail. Then I cut the tail piece [Command+X]. Then I undo the damage to the b character. Next I open the ll slot and paste in the tail piece I just cut. Finally, I close the ll, and with it still selected I type Command+G to get the new version of the component into the clipboard. Now I can copy the component, and paste it into the p slot.

The result makes the problems obvious.

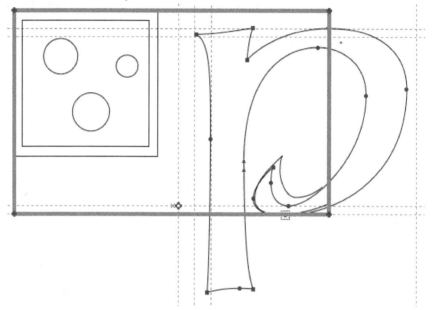

Look at how much larger the tail piece is from the b. In the capture, I've already fixed the upper left of the bowl that was too thin (step four below). Also notice how the dark outline of the component obscures the new tail piece. I go through and fix the flaws.

1. Select the upper half of the character: Move it down to the x-height overshoot.

2. Select the bottom of the stem: move it down to just above the descender line.

3. The stem is too wide: use the ball to fix that.

4. Fix the upper left of the shoulder: The wide point of the bowl is fine.

5. Move the new tail piece into position

6. Deselect the component

7. Use the Knife to cut off the p tail: I make the cut as close as I can to ends of the new tail I'm adding

8.   Double-quick on the old tail to select it and delete it.

9.   Choose Decompose Component from the Edit menu:
marquee and delete the three weight balls

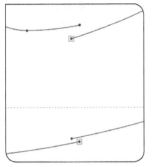

When I enlarge the area where the old and new tails meet I can see what you see to the left. The ends do not meet. But this is no problem at all. This is easy to fix.

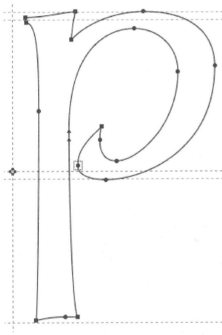

10.   Select the top endpoint of the original bowl: drag it on top of the top endpoint of the new tail. The two points will automatically join and become one.

11.   To clean up the new curve: Marquee the new point and merge [Command+M].

12.   Do the same with the two bottom endpoints: Be sure to merge away the new point added by the joined endpoints.

13.   Paste the component back in: (It will still be available.) Use the weight balls to adjust the width of the new tail

14.   I'm done: I close the p to look at the two new glyphs in the font window. I want to see how they look—and more importantly, do I like that look? When I look at the b & p in the font window they look good.

Fixing the d & q

These work exactly the same way. The only difference is that when I drop in the pieces component, I click on the Flip tool and flip the component. I did have to move the extrema on the sides of the bowl down a bit to get things to look right. But the final products were quick and easy.

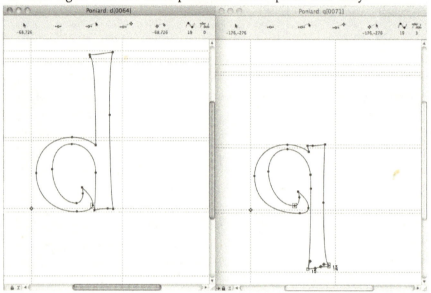

Fixing the h, i, j, k, & l

All I had to do here was move up the upper serif of the h-i-k, lower the top of the stem of the i-j, and narrow the stems a bit. For the k, I had to use the weight balls to make the upper arm thick enough. I made it the minimum.

Fixing the a

This is a character I usually dread. Because it has three horizontals within the x-height, the counters can get too small very quickly. Also there is usually a lot of fussing with the weight balls. When I look at it in the font window it looks a bit wide in comparison with the characters I've already completed. So, I open it and take a look.

The thins are too thin

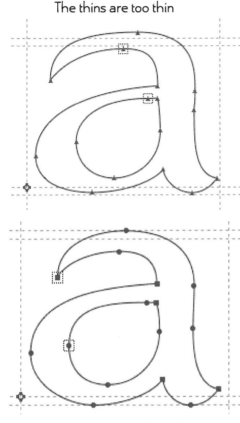

For some reason, all the points are tangent points. I use Clean Up Paths with the Simplify command turned on. This converts all the points to curve and corner, plus it adjusts the extrema a little bit.

Once I actually got into it, everything went well. I suspect that part of this is because Fontographer simply handles paths and auto-curvature very well. I find it to be better than FontLab, FreeHand, Illustrator, or InDesign. I've really enjoyed getting back to the original drawing program.

As I hope you can see, the a has been modified to look a lot more like the look we have been developing in the h, k, & d.

Fixing the n & m

I always build the n off the lowercase h. The first thing I do (in the font window) is select the h and copy it. Then I paste it into the n slot. If I am blessed, the n will be an h with a shortened stem. But that rarely happens. As usual, this was merely a hope. The reality is what you see at the top of the next page.

The process of editing paths is full of these little issues. For example, I found that stretching the top serif up to the descender line was giving me a 100 emu vertical handle length on the corner point of the left serif. Why? Have not a clue. That's why I didn't mention it. But it still needed to be fixed. There were several places where I selected a point and merged it. Try to keep your paths as simple as possible—extrema only, if possible.

The first serif adjustment

As mentioned this made things look horrible. But it is really no big deal. What happened is that the vertical handle off the two points on either side of the stem was not reduced. When you marquee points you do not select those handles.

So I had to grab the handles and move them down. Because the h was finished, the n weight measurements were fine.

To do the m

1. I pasted two copies of the n into the m slot.

2. I selected the points on each that were in the way: I merged them one by one.

I kept everything on the right n except the upper serif. I selected the shoulder and tail to move it to the left until the space between it and the center stem balanced with the space between the left and center stem.

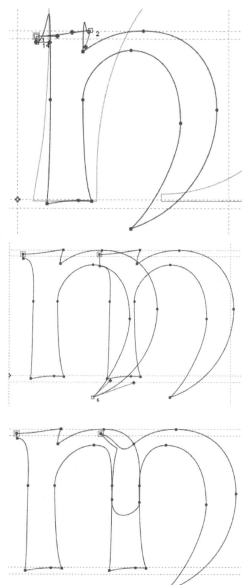

As you can see I matched the overlap for the center stem carefully.

3.   Remove Overlap [Command+Shift+O]: this left a couple of extra points on the center stem.

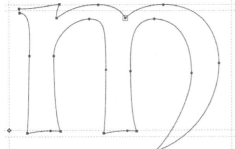

4.   Select and merge those extra points

5.   Clean Up Paths: You should always run this command to make sure the extrema are there.

6.   It's done!

I'm not sure I like the sharpness of the curve on the inner right shoulder left of the center stem. I may come back and fix it later (I did do that). But for now, it looks good.

Fixing the o & c

I start this pair with the o. This is a simple fix with the weight balls and adjusting the size to fit within the x-height overshoots. The only thing I did outside of that was to make it a little more narrow.

Next, I tackled the c. Here I pasted a copy of the o (missing the center dot) over the top of the existing c. Using the Knife, I cut off the right side of the o and the left side of the c. Then I dragged the pieces together.

> **Joining paths (reminder):** Fontographer makes this a joy. All I need to do is drag the end points of two different paths on top of each other. They are automatically joined and I can type Command+M to merge that new point out of existence.

Fixing the e

Here I want to give you some step by step help. The e is considerably more complex. It has the same problems as the a (the three horizontals) with the additional situation caused by the fact that the counter on top needs to be smaller than the counter on the a to keep the e's aperture (the opening below the counter and above the tail) open enough for good readability. I do still want to use the two paths from the o I just fixed to get the weights off on the right track.

1. Paste the o over the e: Here you can see how much has to be changed to make the character work in the new scenario.

    The biggest problem is cutting the old e apart without losing shape of the counter. So the next thing I did was select the old e and move it up so I could cut it without interference.

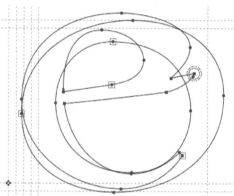

2. Cut the left off the e

3. Cut the right off the o

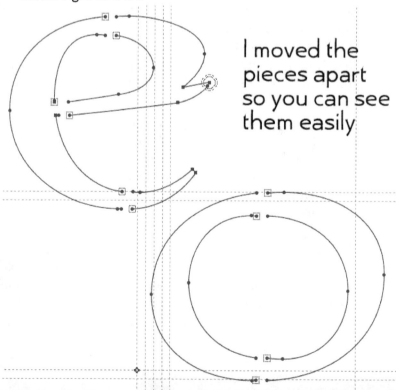

I moved the pieces apart so you can see them easily

4. Delete the spare parts

5. Attach the left of the o to the tail and
   two pieces of the counter of the e

6. Attach the new tail from pieces component to
   the bottom and the counter half to the top

   On a lark, I decided to try to add the tail piece
   from my pieces character. After taking a look I
   like it but it'll take some adjustment to keep it
   from plugging up too bad.

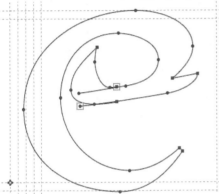

Don't be afraid to experiment

These things aren't the Mona Lisa. It's just a glyph. What you must decide as you experiment is whether it can be done without compromising readability. In this case that is an iffy proposition—especially with the spur coming out of the crossbar in addition to the very unusual crossbar tail inside the bowl. So, I keep things as open as I can.

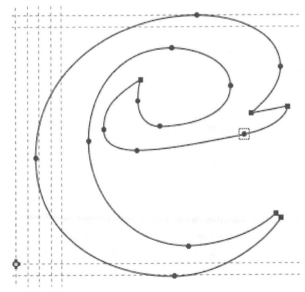

However, in this case, it seems to me that the spur gives the crossbar some grounding to keep the proposed glyph from spinning off in a spiral. Obviously, it is still an e so readability is OK. I'm surprised it works as well as it does and that is really fun.

The finished e is quite pleasing to my eye. I hope you like it. As usual, the new font has a different character and style than I expected. That's why this is so much fun.

Finishing the lowercase

At this point I decided that because this was just a simple modification of an existing font, I would quickly finish the lowercase and move on to the caps. Here's where they ended up (without any letterspacing).

Moving to the caps

Here I start the same way I did for the lowercase.

1. I select the caps

2. I type Command+\ to open the Transform dialog: It's still set at 65% Scale Uniformly.

3. Change that to scale: set the horizontal to 65%. Leave the vertical at 100% My caps heights have not changed much.

4. Begin opening the characters and fixing them with the weight balls

Rather than bore you with all of the character adjustments, let's hold off on that until the next new font coming. At this point, all you need to know is that with everything set up, it took less than three hours to do all the caps.

Moving to the numbers

For this one I need to decide whether I am going to use oldstyle (lowercase) or lining (uppercase) figures (numbers. For most of my fonts, I do OpenType and use both. But for this one we are staying with the old 8-bit, 256 character limit—so, I need to decide. The basic question is: how often will I be setting this font in all caps? My answer is rarely.

I chose oldstyle figures

As a result, I need to transform them the same way I did for the lowercase letters—65% Uniformly.

Tip on the pieces: I found while doing the capital letters that it saved a lot of time to add the pieces to all the glyphs before I started working on them. I use Command+G on the II slot and then I open the Zero, in this case. Command+V pastes the component. Then I type the Next Glyph command [Command+]] which takes me to the next character to the right, and paste again. Then I can just hold down the Command key and type], then v, then], then v, and so on until they all have a copy of the component in them.

It took about a half hour to do the numbers. Now I have to do all the rest of the characters. Let's start with the composite glyphs. These are glyphs made up of two or more characters. The ñ, for example, is made up of two components: the n and the tilde accent character.

Pasting in the components

Next we paste in our components for the accented characters. Some of this you want to do in the font window, some of it needs to be done in the outline window.

What is a component?

A component is a glyph added as a piece to another glyph. Sometimes the component is decomposed to use as parts. I think I covered this briefly earlier. But we need to go over it again. Here are the characteristics:

- It comes in with a 3 point grey frame: If it helps you understand the process, the component is a grouping of the outlines of a character. It can be resized but not edited unless you decompose it. Decomposing releases the paths back to normal.

- ❦ Updating the original updates the component: This is a real asset. But, it's not quite as good as you think. The letterspacing is not updated.

- ❦ Pasting in a component in the font window replaces everything and brings in the letterspacing also: Pasting a component in the font window deletes everything that might already be in that character slot.

- ❦ Pasting a component into an outline window simply adds the component: It does not delete anything or change the letterspacing.

- ❦ Decomposing a component allows you to edit the outline: BUT it will no longer be updated.

- ❦ Accented characters use two components: You paste in the character first to set the letterspacing. Then you paste in the accent and adjust the position.

- ❦ It is easier to build ligatures with components: and then decompose them one at a time as you build them together.

I add the component letters in the font window. For example, I'll select the cap A. Type Command+G to get the component. Then select the composited glyphs that use that component one at a time to paste in the component. This cleans up the glyphs and sets the letterspacing.

I paste in all the As, then all the es, then the Cs, then the Is, and so forth. Once I have all the base characters added, I then add all the acutes into open Outline windows. Then I move on to the graves, and so on. To reword, after I get all the character portions of the composites entered, I then open the individual outline windows and add the accents (or the other parts of the ligature). You will always need to adjust the horizontal position of the accents for the lowercase and the vertical and horizontal position for the caps.

It will be quicker if you add each accent to all the glyphs in which it is used and then go onto the next one.

In other words, add all the grave accents to the caps and lowercase, then all the acutes, and so on. It makes things go more quickly.

No, there is no automation on this. It is slow and very tedious. But! Good news! It really doesn't take all that long. You are only doing 59 of them. You can make all the composited characters in a half hour to forty minutes. So, I guess for me it's just the tedium I dread.

Fixing all the special characters

A lot of this is dependent upon your use. For me, as I will be selling my font, I need to do them all. If you are doing a font for your own use, do the ones that make you happy.

Some suggested special characters

I have some personal quirks—(definitely not used by anyone else) that I recommend. They are useful to me and I have put them in my fonts for nearly two decades now.

- ❦ An open ballot box □: I delete the section character and put this blank check box (□) there. The keystroke is Option+6.

- ❦ A check mark √: I use the square root for this. The keystroke is Option+V.

- ❦ The fancy bullet ◇: I change the lozenge into a fancy bullet. Keystroke: Option+Shift+V

- ❦ Another bullet ∆: I change the delta into another fancy bullet. Option+J

You can play around much more than that. But you need to do stuff you can remember. And it only works for your own fonts. If you start selling fonts, you better stay fairly close to normal (though I include the four mentioned above in all my fonts I sell).

I did do the letterspacing at this point. I used the Auto Space & Auto Kern commands. I've made those instructions into two separate chapters as we go through designing the next font, CushingTwo. Fontographer makes that a breeze.

In addition, I have added Appendix A which talks about serious hand letterspacing, as necessary.

So, it's done!

I adjusted all the characters. I've checked all the letterspacing—at least good enough to get going with testing. So, what I need to do is generate the font files and test them for a couple of weeks. That way I can make sure that the spacing works and there is no glitch.

Generate font files

Simply choose the command from the File menu. Choose Cross-platform (Mac, Windows, Unix) and your choice of .otf or .ttf. In my case, I do both.

Then install your font.

ABCDEFGHIJKLMNOPQRSTUVWXYZ
AaBbCcDdEeGgHhKkMmOoPpRrSsUuWw9y
1234567890abcdefghijklmnopqrstuvwxyz
It seems to work fine! So far...

Moving on: a new font

Every font has a starting point. This time I am going to work on a font I've wanted to do for many years. James Felici reminded me of the font in an article he wrote for Creative Pro in January 2011 called *Type History: What a Difference a Century Makes*. He had a scan of the font there. It is called Cushing No. 2, and it looks like this.

CHARMING PRESENT
Most splendid fur carnival
that ever stirred this town
is now taking place at our
newly enlarged emporium
RECORD BREAKING SALE
Finest quartered oak easy chairs
with a ton of comfort in every inch
are now displayed for the approval
of our customers. Come and look
them over some day 1234567890

Now, I agree that a lot of this looks pretty old-fashioned—but that can be fixed. The good news, for me, is that I have tried to do this before and never got it done. But I do have some pieces I can use to start. The first attempt is a pretty font I called Bushing & released in January 2011.

I started this time by printing an enlarged copy of the scan. I drew on the dimension lines and measured them. This will give me my percentages for my dimensions.

If I divide things out, I get the following dimensions:

❦ Ascender: 820

❦ X-height: 545

❦ Descender: 180

That seems a little bit extreme for me and my taste. So I am going to go with the following dimensions as I set up the new font file.

❦ Ascender: 800

❦ Cap height: 750

❦ X-Height: 540

❦ Descender: 200

I've decided to name the font CushingTwo. With that I'm ready to get started.

Setting up the font

Wanting an OpenType font this time, I start with a template I made. You can have a copy of it if you go to my Website at hackberry-fonts.com. Just follow the Fontographer link. It's called the Second Template. It is in a zipped folder containing the FOG file and a OpenType feature file.

This font is set up to show you many things you need to do to make an OpenType font with small caps and old-style figures (lowercase numbers). At this point you do not need to worry about any of that. I left the caps, lowercase, and numbers in the template for us to use in this exercise.

Font Information

I name this font CushingTwo and use Book for the weight. Then I add the dimensions we just decided upon. Feel free to modify this to work for you. Once I add the dimension and click OK, I save the font as CushingTwo.fog into a new folder I make to hold everything in my 2011 folder in my fonts folder on my hard drive. This makes things easy to back up into my backup hard drive at the end of the work day—every day.

Add the guides

I added guides for the cap height and x-height, plus the overshoots as we did for Poniard. In addition I added three vertical guides to the left side at 20 emus, 45 emus, and 75 emus. They are just there as a result of my habits in working in FontLab, but I thought you might want an explanation for them as they appear in all the captures.

Basic letterspacing to start

As you begin to do the characters of a font, simply add about 30 emus to the left and right of the side extrema of the character. Auto Space will take care of the rest. If you are doing a font that needs more careful hand spacing, please read Appendix A.

Doing the caps

In this case, I simply adjusted the caps. In the process I got the pieces slot set up the way I want it set up. I started with the cap I and the lowercase l.

Doing the I & l

I decide to use the cap I and lowercase l as is. I move them so the left edge of the stem lines up with the 75 emus vertical guide. But other than that I make no changes. For you, if you are following along, this is the point where you first take a look at the serifs and decide if you like them or not. If not this is where you begin to bring them into line with your visions for your version of the font.

Setting up my design pieces: ll slot

In the template, I have added an ll character at the very end slot. If you click on it, and open the Outline window, you'll see it has a set of the Bushing pieces used to design that font. In that glyph slot I place my weight balls, my serif pieces, and other pieces as needed. The problem is that I am going to modify them quite a bit.

So, the first thing I do is delete the pieces from Bushing. As mentioned, I begin work with the cap I and the lowercase l. These will provide me with the new serifs I need.

I add two cutting guidelines: These are arbitrary, but the locations you see to the right work fine.

I add the serif pieces by pasting in first the I and then the l.

With the Knife, I cut across on the cutting guidelines: I hold down the shift key to keep a perfectly horizontal cut.

I move the serif pieces into position as you see: Make sure you move them with the left and right arrow keys only. I eventu-

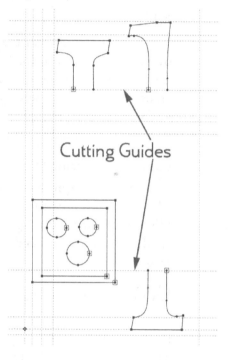

Cutting Guides

ally moved everything to the left of the Origin point. It is important that they retain their alignment with the cutting guides. This will make adding the serifs to the characters much easier.

Later I picked up the maximum and minimum weight balls from the cap O: I added them to the ll slot. But look at what happened as I worked my way to the lowercase.

 Major redo! I just made a substantial change of mind: This is not unusual. It will not be unusual for you either, so I thought I would tell you about it. I was blithely going along. I'd just finished up the caps and was starting the lowercase. Suddenly, I looked at the font window

and glanced over at the Cushing No. 2 sample I have
taped to my shelving next to my monitor. It looked too
dark for a book version (to my eye). So I made it more
narrow. This necessitated adding a third weight ball,
redoing all the serif pieces, and readjusting all the
caps I thought I had finished.

You must keep checking yourself to see if you are
matching your vision. It is incredibly easy to wander off and
do quite a bit of work until your eye notices that you have
done this horrible thing. There is nothing to do but fix it.

 Production tip: As mentioned for Poniard,
another thing that had been bothering me
was the fact that the edge of the weight
balls were always being covered by the thick grey line
found around an imported component. This is where
I discovered the benefit of putting a box around the
weight balls. This has completely solved the problem
and greatly speeds up my adjustments.

As mentioned, I did need to go through all the caps
and readjust them. However, because it had already been
done once, the readjustments took less than 15 minutes for
all 26 caps. However, the changes in the lowercase are quite
bit more extensive. I won't bore you with them all. But let's
look at some of them at least.

I realize that my order of working may appear arbitrary
to you, but believe me it is not. The reason we are starting with the C&lc plus numbers is simple. When we start
making the composites, the letterspacing from the components will be added to the composited figures. This saves a
lot of time in production (unless you are auto spacing).

The same is true of all the special characters. For
example, when we get to the assembly of the dollar sign, we
will first add an S component. This will set the letterspacing, then we will add a slash. The adjustments to the two
pieces to make the dollar sign will be within the confines of
letterspacing that is already set—saving a lot of production
time while maintaining consistency.

It is the little things like this that will get your production up to the place where you can create a font quickly
enough to avoid that dreaded, "I'm tired of this," where you
never actually get the font done.

More complex ll glyphs

I thought I'd share what I am using for a new font I
am developing to use for my book designs. I call it Libro. In
this one I needed five weight balls: stem, arm and serif
widths, plus a maximum and minimum for curved counters.
I also added a large X rotated to show me the axis used for
those max and min weights. The final ll glyph looks like this
(so far). I do have another glyph for small cap weights.

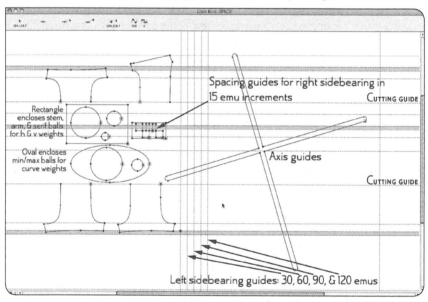

I colored the overshoots to help you locate things. As you
may notice, this is also set up to do professional handspac-
ing in FontLab after the font is complete [see Appendix A].

Developing a work style

As I look at this portion, it seems that it would be
good to mention the different normal work styles you'll each

develop. My goal here is to share some things I've learned while you put your working style together.

Every font is different, but I have developed some character strings that make sense to me. These observations are certainly not rigid. The goal is to develop a procedure that gets you as quickly as possible to the actual look and style you will use for your font. I'll cover this in more detail in the design chapter near the end of the book. This is always a process under development when you start a new font. I usually do the characters in this order.

Basic weight and serif style

Cap I, J, & H: This gives me a good feel for the weight of the vertical stems and the basic serif design. Even for the sans serif fonts, the ends of the stem are usually slightly asymmetrical and cupped in some fashion. This is where I make my first letterspacing decisions.

Modulation and axis

Cap O, Q, C,& G: Doing these four characters enables me to decide upon the modulation. This is where I develop the weight balls and axis.

Modulation and axis, plus lower right serif

Lowercase l, h, n, m, & r: Here I see if the axis decisions and modulation are going to work for me on this font. I decide how the shoulder is going to come out of the stem. I also take a look at how I will modify the bottom serif on the right stem. If that is really distinctive I add it as a piece to my ll slot as I did the swash in Poniard.

First inkling of punctuation

Lowercase i & j: The only interesting part of these characters is that they usually begin the design of my . , ; & : glyphs. But I don't put the punctuation together until after the basic 62 characters are done.

Lowercase o, c, & e: By now things are getting into a rhythm.
Cap P, R, & B: I usually make the upper bowls the same for these three (though many think the P bowl should be larger),
Lowercase b & q then d & p: The similarities here are obvious.

Slanted upper serifs

Cap V, W, & Y: Here I need to deal with the slanted upper serifs. Depending on the font, I sometimes add these to the pieces glyph also.

Lowercase v, w, & y: I take the decisions I just made and apply them to these three characters.

By now I have over half of the basic 52 characters designed. The look of the font is established. I find that it really helps to have these designed when I get to work on the more tricky characters like the K, S, X, g, k, s, and x. To finish the concept, I find that the basic 62 are needed before I start on characters like the &, $, ¢, £, µ, ¥, Ω, €, And all the rest. As you can see many of these characters are built directly off one or more of the basic 62 glyphs: A–Z, a–z, and one through zero.

Doing the lowercase

While we are discussing all of this, I have finished the caps, as mentioned. I've also put together the characters built off the lowercase l—namely the k, i, j, and h. The h naturally led into the development of the n and m.

Then I went through the o, c, e progression. For some reason, I usually go from here to the g even though that character is unique in all my fonts. But for this font I followed the advice written above and went to the bqdp glyphs.

You simply need to cover them all. The key is to get the alphabet complete before you move on to the more esoteric characters. The other important aspect of this is consistency. This is why I have emphasized the weight balls so much. They are the key to keeping a consistent look throughout the font.

Fixing the lowercase b

As you can see below, I've already made quite a few changes to the paths of the b. I lowered the x-height to match the new setup. I did quite a bit of weight ball work to get the thicknesses fixed. I took the knife at my upper cutting guideline and sliced off the old serif & deleted it.

You can also see, I have moved the upper serif in the pieces component to align with the upper cut line. I have it set up straddling the stem to help attach the new serif. I decompose the pieces component. Then I delete all the component pieces I do not need.

The reason for the cutting guides

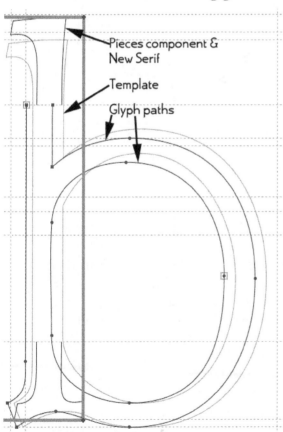

Pieces component & New Serif

Template

Glyph paths

One of the wonderful things about Fontographer is the fact I have mentioned many times already—that when you put the endpoint of one path on top of the end point of another path, they automatically join, merge, whatever you want to call it.

By using the cutting guide when I cut off the upper serif, the two cut off ends were exactly on the cutting guide, Moreover, they are set at the same width as the serif piece in the component. So, to attach the serif all I had to do was move the serif piece sideways with the arrow keys. As soon as they came within range (the snap-to setting in preferences), the endpoints merged. Now all I need to do is marquee the two points you see in the capture to the right and type Command+M to merge them.

So, the b is now completed. I will now go through the rest of the lowercase and get them all adjusted. It is the same procedure as we went through for Poniard. It is the same procedure for every font.

Moving to the d

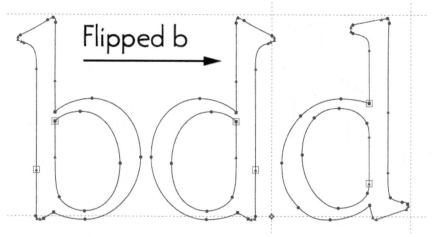

Flipped b ⟶

This is a place where you need to be thankful that I am giving you a start. While it may be true that you can simply flip a b when dealing with a monoline sans, that is certainly not true anywhere else. Let me quickly remind you of the obvious issues. Because CushingTwo has a very slight modulation, I've used Adobe Caslon to show the problems more clearly.

As you can see clearly here, if you are drawing a font from scratch, there are huge adjustments required in the modulation. One of the reasons I am giving you a starting place is so we can get through this process more quickly enabling us to discuss issues like letterspacing early enough in the book to help you in the design process.

 Notice the top serifs: Some of the things you quickly notice when looking at an old font like Caslon are the inconsistencies. I imagine that most of you noticed that the top serif on the b is very different from the top serif on the d. My question is: How many of you noticed that the axis is slightly different in the two characters? It is these inconsistencies that give Caslon much of its visual interest. This is why you need to develop your inner sense of right and wrong and keep things loose.

If you do not like my serifs or weight decisions

I probably should have mentioned this before I got this far. But I am assuming that you are doing your own thing with these fonts. Set up the dimensions, weights, and serif design according to your sense of taste. It will do you no good to blindly follow my lead.

My intent is to attempt to answer your questions as you get to them in your designs. But I certainly do not want you to duplicate my efforts. That would be theft and violate the copyright of CushingTwo. But then that only matters if you are going to be selling your work. My suggestion is to wait a while on that until you have a good design of your own. This is supposed to be fun, remember?

A basic procedure

Make as many of your design decisions before you start as you possibly can.

- ❦ Start with the lowercase l: and adjust the height and weight. Redraw the serifs until they make you happy—or eliminate them. You can certainly make the terminals sans serif.

- ❦ Next go to the cap O: and set up the height, axis, and modulation. If you are only doing a monoline sans serif, you'll obviously only need one weight ball. If you have any modulation, you'll need two. If you add an axis you'll need the three weight balls: minimum, maximum, and stem weights.

You may want to add an axis line: If I am going to be using a relatively rigid axis, I often draw a very thin rectangle and rotate it to the correct angle. I make it higher than the cap height and down to the descender line (so I can set the minimums in the descenders). I then rotate a copy 90°. For many fonts, the axis varies from character to character. Carefully examine your inspiration. For CushingTwo the modulation is slight and varies, but it is your choice.

- ❦ Then do the cap I: to get the top serif for the caps. It is very important that you move it sideways with the arrow keys so that it will automatically join to the stem stubs.

One of the things I have started to do as I work through these adjustments to the basic 62 characters is paste a pieces component in each one. This really helps me keep track of what I have done and what I still have to fix. In addition, it lets me freely copy/paste in pieces to use without forcing me to go to the font window to put the pieces component back into the clipboard.

On the next page you can see at a glance that I have done the caps. Plus I have completed the lowercase from the a to the e. It's really hard to miss the component. They make it really obvious whether you have completed a glyph or not. The only issue is that a really wide character like a W or M will not show the component (if you have moved them to the left of the origin point). It will be hidden off to the left. All you will see is that the W is off center. So, you still need to go through all the characters to double-check.

Always be thinking of ways to be more efficient. It will help with your consistency.

,	-	.	/	0	1	2	3	4	5	6
				0	1	2	3	4	5	6

7	8	9	:	;	<	=	>	?	@	A
7	8	9								A

B	C	D	E	F	G	H	I	J	K	L
B	C	D	E	F	G	H	I	J	K	L

M	N	O	P	Q	R	S	T	U	V	W
M	N	O	P	Q	R	S	T	U	V	W

X	Y	Z	[	\	]	^	_	`	a	b
X	Y	Z							a	b

c	d	e	f	g	h	i	j	k	l	m
c	d	e	f	g	h	i	j	k	l	m

n	o	p	q	r	s	t	u	v	w	x
n	o	p	q	r	s	t	u	v	w	x

y	z	{	|	}	~	Ä	Å	Ç	É
y	z								

Finishing the lowercase

With all of this prep work, knocking off the lowercase was a breeze. It took a little over an hour to put together the lowercase. The fun part was deciding what to use from the image I have of Cushing No. 2. All sorts of little anomalies started appearing as I noticed them. For example, the a and the r both had ball terminals—and the one on the r was huge. (I didn't use that. It seemed out of character for my vision of the font.) The g had a sharp point in the join between the upper and lower bowls (I liked that and used it). The s actually had beaks that were nothing like the other terminals.

One of the really nice tools in Fontographer is the ability to quickly print off a proof of selected glyphs. I did that above with the newly "finished" C&lc. I did them at 67 point in this case, but it is only important that they are large enough for you to see clearly. You simply select the glyphs you want to look at, type Command+P, select a point size, and print.

ABCDEFGHIJKLMNO PQRSTUVWXYZabc defghijklmnopqrstu vwxyz

The work of design

In all of these things I had to make decisions and compromises. I'm not interested in a historical reproduction. I'm trying for a "look" that is consistent with my reaction to what I see when looking at the two set paragraphs of Cushing No. 2 in my sample.

What do I like about the look of that font? That's a tough question. This is where my solution will be different than yours—even if you also like Cushing no. 2. I like the feeling of openness, the roundness, and the large x-height—among other things.

However, my version is slightly condensed which messes up the roundness a bit. You must be constantly pulling back and looking at the font as a whole. As I held the proof in my hand, it was immediately obvious that simply rotating the p & q from the b & d had caused a little problem. The outside extrema of the bowls in the b & d were a bit above the centerline of the bowl. As a result, my p & q definitely looked like they were sagging. I simply selected the extrema and moved them up a little with the arrow key.;

The next thing I noticed was that the lowercase a was no longer the delight it is in the original. In my efforts to "regularize" the font a bit, I had lost some of the character. I still believe that the a in Cushing No. 2 is too extreme and far too "old-fashioned", but I need to go a bit further with my revision. The original is very much outside the look of the rest of the font with the drooping top curve and the large curved bottom serif. I still want the aperture much more open and the large curving bottom serif is found nowhere else in the sample. But I can get the look closer to the new feel. Hopefully you agree that I did that with the second revision.

First attempt   Cushing #2   Second attempt

There were several other things I saw and quickly fixed while examining the quick proof. The s was a bit squared off. The serif on the arm of the k was too dark. The upper bowl of the g bothered me. Little things like that.

The key is to design the font as a whole

Individual glyphs can look really nice yet be quite outside the general look of the font. That's what I am dealing with in the lowercase a. That was cute and quirky at the turn of the 20th century. It's no longer considered cool in the new millennium.

On the other hand, quirky has been the fashion recently in many fields. There is nothing wrong with that. But one weird letter does not make a quirky font. As you refine the vision for your font, make sure everything fits that overall style

I often do the numbers next

However, to help you conceptually, I will delay that a little. What is important now is to realize that you really must do the basic letterspacing of the 52 characters we have completed so far. This needs to be done before your begin compositing the accented glyphs. You will find that it also helps a lot to have the letterspacing decisions in your mind as you do the numbers and build the special characters— especially the ligatures.

Letterspacing

I want to start with a quote from an older book that was recommended to me by Thomas Phinney, now of Extensis: Stephen Moye's *Fontographer: Type by Design*. It gets pretty technical in places, and it is out of print now.

- ❦ "Interior spaces: are helpful in establishing the overall spacing of a font

- ❦ "Exterior spaces: are used to judge the spacing between two of more specific letterforms

- ❦ "Principal shapes (like stems): are used to judge letterspacing. Serifs, when present, are used to *confirm* good letterspacing

- ❦ "Spacing: is both typeface-dependent & size-dependent"

- ❦ "(Centering): "The mathematical center of a letterform will rarely coincide with the optical center"

This book has given me a better handle on talking about letterspacing. It's out of print, but it has very good information. Much of the information in the letterspacing portions of this book I originally learned from Stephen's book while writing my FontLab book.

 Please bear with me a little bit: I'll give the fun and easy solution in a bit. For now you need to understand the theory a little—simply to help you understand what you see in the Outline windows.

Professional letterspacing: At this point, I simply need to tell you the truth. Fontographer is designed for experienced graphic designers who want to do a font for fun. Letterspacing is not fun. Fontographer has excellent tools if you need to get serious about it. I will show you how to do advanced hand letterspacing in Appendix A. The good news is that you do not need them. Fontographer has good automatic letterspacing. My assumption is that almost all of you will be satisfied by the automatic capabilities. Even if you see the problems, in InDesign you can simply use Optical Kerning. Some fonts are simply problematic. We will discuss professional letterspacing in Appendix A, as mentioned.

Looking at letterspacing conceptually

First, let's look at these concepts. We need to understand where we start. Letterspacing must be complete before starting the kerning. Before you can do that, we need to go through several word and concept definitions.

Letterspacing: This sets up the normal spacing for all the characters in the font.

Kerning: This is taken care of after the letterspacing is set to deal with individual spacing issues between letter pairs

Ligatures: When building them, you need to check closely to make sure the internal spacing of them matches the finished spacing of the entire font.

The beginnings of letterspacing should be done by hand and eye: As suggested, even if you are going to automate, you need to start out with even, minimal space on both sides of your characters. Fontographer does automate spacing, but you still need to check carefully. You need to generate a test font to try it out. There are simply too many variables. This can only be done by the trained and experienced eye. I cannot tell you the rights and wrongs. It is all determined by your taste, style, experience, and judgement. Even the automatic spacing requires some experience.

What is the goal?

In an excellent font, the characters fit very evenly and smoothly. This character fit is called letterspacing. This is your responsibility. Beyond that is a very careful use of spacing throughout your documents, in general. This is the job of the page layout specialist. Even excellent fonts will not help a word processor or a careless typesetter. The first and one of the most important attributes of excellent type is the smoothness of the color of the type. What is called the *type color* is created by the design of the font character shapes, the spacing of those characters, the spacing of the words, the leading between the lines of type, and the paragraph spacing.

Smooth type color must be one of your major concerns for letterspacing

Professional type should have an even color when seen from far enough away so that the body copy can no longer be read and becomes gray shapes. Squinting your eyes until the type blurs can also do this for you with practice. You will come to see that this even type color is imperative. It is what allows the control of the reader's eye you need for clear and comfortable communication. You will learn to print proofs of typical copy to keep your type as smooth as possible. This smooth gray background is the starting point of excellent typography and readability. Smooth type color must be one of your major concerns.

The decisions needed for good letter fit

Consistency: This is what I have always taught. The areas between the letters need to be consistent. Stephen uses the analogy of pouring an equal volume of sand between the letters to fill up the spaces. Whatever works for you to understand this, you need to get a grasp of this concept.

The real problem comes when we start to deal with issues like the counter space in a c as compared to the smaller interior space of an e and an o with none of that.

An absolute amount of space: Here we get into some of the decisions that you will be making that involve your sense of style, tradition, font classification, and font size. The problem here is that display type (24 point and larger usually) needs far less spacing than text type (9–12 point). So first we must decide the primary use of the font we are designing.

If it is a text font: This is set surprisingly loose—using it for display purposes will require designers using your font to tighten the tracking.

If it is a display font: If you set it up for very large sizes (36 point and above) radically loosening the tracking will probably be necessary for text use (if text use is even possible with your display fonts).

For caps & small caps: increased spacing is required—usually a bit more for the small caps.

To quote Moye again:

"The amount of spacing is a function of good taste, while consistency is a matter of skill"

Again, the good news is that Fontographer has very good auto spacing capabilities. Even so, you will need to work on both aspects throughout your career. In addition, your taste will change throughout your career so your spacing values will change also. I am a child of the '70s & '80s typographically, so I tend to like my x-heights large and my spacing tight. That is no longer the fashion. Your tastes are going to be different than mine. They are also going to vary from font to font.

Display or Text?

Letterspacing changes with the point size. In fact, if you have read any of my books on formatting, you realize that leading varies a lot with point size also. What is necessary spacing for ten point body copy looks absolutely humongous at seventy-two point.

It naturally follows that text faces—those designed to be used for formatting body copy—need quite a bit more letterspacing than display fonts that will be used only for larger headlines and subheads. Unlike hand spacing where you are forced to deal with actual measurements between every letter and every letter pair, Fontographer only requires the choice of a single number. Professional type designers cringe in horror at the thought.

Auto-spacing in Fontographer

Do not do this if you are going to hand space

I wouldn't suggest this unless I thought Fontographer did a pretty good job, and it does. The process is very simple. Go under the Metrics window to Auto Space. When the dialog box opens, click on the Advanced button. It is not that advanced and Easy is simply not good enough.

In the advanced form of the dialog, you have three pages. Here we are doing preliminary spacing. So first, select the caps and lowercase characters.

Spacing

Here we have a slider. You will need to try various figures in the field, but 65 seems to work the best for me for CushingTwo. For a text face with larger serifs, I would probably end up at 75 or 80. For Poniard, I used 55.

Glyphs

Here your selection are determined by where you are in the process. At this point we have just done the C&lc characters. So, for both first letter and second letter I would choose "Glyphs selected in the Font window". When the font is complete, I select various choices depending on what I have done in the font.

| Spacing | Glyphs | Technique |

First Letter: ⦿ All glyphs

      ○ Upper case, lower case, numbers, punctuation

      ○ These glyphs:

      ○ Glyphs selected in the Font window

Second Letter: ⦿ All glyphs

      ○ Upper case, lower case, numbers, punctuation

      ○ These glyphs:

      ○ Glyphs selected in the Font window

Technique

Here the three options vary, depending on where you are in the process. But I normally have it set up as you see above. When we talk about Auto Kern, you'll see I usually set the threshold there at 10%. If that is the case with you, the threshold here should be the same.

Auto Space

Auto Spacing Mode: ○ Easy   ⦿ Advanced

| Spacing | Glyphs | Technique |

Options: ☐ Monospace numerals

      ☑ Adjust left sidebearings

      ☑ Allow negative right sidebearings

Threshold: 20 ↕

Spacing Direction: Spread and Tighten Glyphs ↕

Spacing Technique: HIO Examine Weighted Average ↕

Weight Minimum By: 20% ↕

(Cancel) (Space)

The Direction and Technique should be set as you see above. This is not the default and this is another reason why you need to use Advanced. *Examine Weighted Average* tries to take into consideration factors like the interior space of a c, two tall stems like lk, two bowls like bo, and the point of the tail of the R or k.

Click Space and you're done.

At this point I would do no more. We will re-space later as necessary.

If you are going to sell your fonts

For professional consumption, you really need careful hand spacing of the entire font. I hate to say it, but this should be started as you design the characters. It's a tedious process no matter what. But, doing hand spacing in Fontographer is not too bad. It does take some knowledge and setup, but that is covered in Appendix A.

Carefully examine Appendix A

If you want professional letterspacing, you need to set up your left sidebearing guides and develop a measuring tool as suggested in the appendix. Then finishing off your spacing and adding the kerning will proceed as efficiently as possible.

Accents (diacritics) and composites

Dealing with the diacritics is a small thing, to most of us with our English arrogance, but one you need to take seriously. It is simple politeness to offer the accents in the standard ASCII slots. Part of the problem of designing the accents is that they are scattered all over the font window. So, I thought we'd run through the components and talk briefly about how they are made.

There is rarely an absolute right or wrong

The problem is that the reader must perceive the marks as falling within the normal range. That is difficult to know for those of us who do not use these marks in the languages we speak. Again, the best course of action is to look at the usage in other fonts—especially those within the same font style classification as the one we are designing.

Basic design issues for accents

There are three main problems.

1. The location: accents must be located very precisely. If they are off even a slight bit, the reader will notice. Vertically, lowercase case accents must fit within the ascender or descender space. Cap accents are a real problem. Technically you need to redesign your caps with accents so that the composited glyphs do not extend above the em square. I guess one of my failings as a font designer is that I do not bother with that.

2. The weight: Diacritics must appear to be the same weight as the rest of the font. In truth, they are quite a bit lighter. But they must look "right" [I know that's a real help ;-)]. You must be careful (especially with text fonts) that they do not

disappear at smaller point sizes. This can be an exceptional problem with a diacritic like the ring.

3. The fit: It is important that accents do not touch or overlap preceding or following characters in a word.

A special character the dotless i

For this character slot, you just paste in the lowercase i component to get the metrics, decompose, and delete the dot. It is necessary for all the lowercase accented i glyphs which use a mark centered over the top.

Centered marks

This is a serious issue because you can rarely use the measured or mathematical center of a glyph. For curves like the o, I center the accent over the extrema on the top. This is commonly off-center to the right of the mathematical center.

These problems are increased when the accents are used with a character that is radically different top and bottom. For example, if you are including the Central Europeans in your market, you will have accents above and below the DdGgK-kLlRrSsTt and more. An accent over an r is centered over the curve of the arm. An accent below the r is centered under the stem. An accent over a d is centered over the bowl (except for the comma accent which is moved up to the right of the stem).

> **If you want to get into this more deeply read:** *Problems of diacritic design for Latin script typefaces* **by J. Victor Gaultney or visit:** http://ilovetypography.com/2009/01/24/on-diacritics/ for an article on supporting other languages

Keep them clean

This is not a place for serifs or flourishes. They need to look "normal"—though there is certainly room for style innovation and modulation. As usual, we are dependent upon your innate and learned sense of style and taste. Make sure there is enough space between the letter and accent so they do not visually join at the smaller sizes (unless, of course, you are talking about the cedilla or ogonek which are extensions of the letter shape). Mainly you simply need to take the design of these little marks seriously.

Styling is not a sin

I definitely recommend that you modify your diacritic designs to make them fit within the style vision of your font. You simply need to be careful that the reader will perceive them as normal. We font designers can easily be carried away by designs we love yet the reader cannot comprehend them easily while reading.

Asymmetrical offset marks

Acute ´ é OPTICAL CENTER TOP: ASYMMETRIC OFFSET

Angled somewhere between 30° and 60° From the top right to the bottom left. The top is heavier.

Grave ` à OPTICAL CENTER TOP: ASYMMETRIC OFFSET

This is normally a flipped acute. But it is commonly a little closer to horizontal.

Acute & grave alignment: This depends on several factors. These accents are offset. The lower tip of the accent is typically centered on the visual center of the glyph. But that is true only if the accent is more vertical with a 60° angle or higher. If they are relatively flat [30°], then they are centered on the line separating the lower third and the upper two thirds of the mark. Other slopes are adjusted between those extremes.

Optically centered marks

As mentioned, I center these over the extrema of the curve or bowl. But you always need to look carefully and adjust it to fit your sense of normal. This recognition of normalcy will take a while to develop by looking the widely varying solutions of fonts you like—designed by foundries you trust. Most important is a consistent placement throughout the font. This is especially true of the vertical location. I set mine up with a guide for the lowercase and then move them up as needed for the caps.

Circumflex ^ Î OPTICAL CENTER TOP

More or less a vertically flipped v, but the legs are often spread out and the apex is commonly flat for the capital letters. Be careful not to make it too wide. The width of the e is a good guide to that. You may want to make it more narrow to work over the dotless i.

Diaeresis ¨ ö OPTICAL CENTER TOP

This is also the umlaut in other languages. One is a matter of emphasis, The other actually changes the sound of the letter (umlaut, I think). These two dots should be the same width as the circumflex. I usually use the style of the period in the font. For the letters I&i, the dots are commonly moved together—but that means you need to decompose the component.

Tilde ˜ ñ OPTICAL CENTER TOP

This is a little squiggle, the same width as the circumflex. It curves up on the left and down on the right. It should look level, angled neither up nor down.

Ring ° Å OPTICAL CENTER TOP

This is a smaller version of the degree symbol. The trick is to get it dark enough to look like it belongs to the font without completely plugging up in smaller sizes. It is commonly attached to the apex of the A.

Caron ˇ Ž OPTICAL CENTER TOP

This is a flipped Circumflex. But remember to flip it horizontally as well if the accent is modulated.

Breve ˘

This is the same basic shape as the caron but with a curve point instead of a corner point at the bottom of the curves. It should be a smooth curve and can be very elegant when modulated.

Dot · OPTICAL CENTER TOP

This is usually a period moved into position.

Cedilla ¸ç OPTICAL CENTER BOTTOM

I tend to make mine too cupped as you can see above. In fact, I just discovered that this glyph in Buddy (the font above) is badly misaligned. I need to go fix it.

Macron ⁻ ā OPTICAL CENTER TOP

This is a minus glyph moved up into the standard accent location. You may need to shorten it a little. It is not included in our composited characters unless you are supporting Eastern European languages.

Double acute ʺ OPTICAL CENTER TOP

This is two acutes side by side as this name implies. The only confusion for me is that FontLab tends to call this glyph the hungarumlaut (which I have always assumed meant that the Magyars used it for their language, but we never covered that when I learned Hungarian for the Air Force ;-).

Ogonek ˛ ę CAREFULLY HAND PLACED

The ogonek is fun to design. It requires precise placement. It is not an accent. Let me quote from Adam Twardoch's website (Google ogonek Twardoch):

> "Ogonek is probably one of the most misunderstood and misshaped character elements ever. It all starts with the essentially wrong assumption that ogonek is an accent. No, it's not. It's much more a character element, just like a stem, a serif or a descent. In a

vast majority of cases ogonek should be smoothly connected with the base glyph, it should be a part of the glyph.... Ogonek is used in Polish and Lithuanian. A similar shape can be also found in the Navajo and Tuchtone languages... It should be noted that the Polish and Lithuanian traditions in drawing the ogonek differ... Ogonek should be a significant element of the letter. In most cases it should reach the descent line."

He goes on to say that the ogonek needs to have the same weight structure as the rest of the font. If you go to Adam's page on the ogonek, you'll see many gorgeous examples. For us, it is just an "accent" to drop in a slot set up to receive it.

There are many more diacritic marks

The Unicode Standard 3.0 includes 82 of these marks. You can choose from the encodings popup menu to add all the glyphs for different languages.

Special composited characters

There are several letters in the basic 8-bit fonts that are used only for specific languages of which you might not be aware. I have seen these glyphs used by Hollywood or TV designers just for a bit of visual excitement (a Buffy the Vampire Slayer billboard using an Eth, as I recall).

Two Icelandic letters needed

Eth Ð ð and Thorn Þ þ

These two letters are included in the standard 8-bit fonts. They will be in the top row, if you are using the Mac OS Roman layout.

Thorn: This glyph is made by combining the cap I and cap p. You lower the bowl of the P until it is centered vertically in the cap height and then composite that with the cap I. For a serif glyph delete both serifs on the cap P.

The lowercase thorn: here you composite the l and the p. You normally need to delete the top serif of the p and the bottom serif of the l to make it work.

Eth: This is a cap D with the en dash moved to the same height as the H crossbar. The bar sticks out on the left about as far as the serif or to the minimum left sidebearing guide you are using for the font. Inside the bowl, you need to be sure you do not fill the bowl, making it an illegible blob. It needs to have the same weight as the rest of the font when typeset with it.

The lowercase eth: This character is slightly difficult. It is not built from a d, but an o. Some try to add the right paren shape), but that rarely fits right. It needs to be a strong, confident arc with a slanted crossbar. The crossbar needs to stay within the width of the glyph—especially on the right side.

Æ, æ, Ø, ø, Œ, and œ

These glyphs are part of many languages. I can find no rules on how to put them together. For example, the Æ ligature commonly keeps the E stem vertical. This leaves the thin stem of the A hanging out in the breeze—often nearly disappearing because of its inherent thinness. As you can see in the subhead of this little section. I tend to lean this center stem to the left a bit.

For the lowercase æ, there's the question of what to do with the bottom of the stem of the a? If you get rid of it, the glyph tends to look almost cut in two. If you leave it, the bottom of the ligature can get weirdly bumpy.

The oslashes simply have readability problems caused by the slash plugging the counter. For very black fonts, I have been known to cut out the center of the slash to leave the counter open. It still seems to read OK.

What is the most common ligature?

The ampersand: This began life as a ligature of the e and t, or et, which is Latin for *and*. Keeping that historical tie to the glyph origins is a good thing, as far as I am concerned. There is a lot of room here for strong stylistic statements.

Currency glyphs & other specialities

Some seem to be simple, like:

The Euro: as a combination of the C and the equal. But the bars ends are normally slanted to the top right a bit. Technically, it is defined as a cap C with a double crossbar.

The dollar: is an S plus a slash, or is it two slashes? Make it fancy. There are no specific rules here. You may well want to eliminate the portion of the slash that overlaps the s-shape itself as it plugs the counters severely.

The sterling (pound) symbol: has always been my nemesis. It is a difficult character to make pretty. Technically, it is defined as a calligraphic cap L with a crossbar. The top of the stem curls over.

The yen: is a cap Y with two crossbars over the lower half of the glyph.

The florin: is a swash calligraphic f.

The cent symbol: is a lowercase c plus a slash.

The dagger: is a cross with a tapering stem. I usually use it to hold a cross to use when needed. So, I eliminate the taper.

The pilcrow, or paragraph symbol: is a flipped P plus an I joined at the top by a bar—or not. It started as a flipped P with a filled bowl. There are so many variations here that you need to just go around the various fonts and look.

The list goes on and on.

If you have any questions about the others, go to typophile.com and ask. But most of them can just be taken from any font and modified to fit your font's style. You do need to do all of them, however, if you plan to sell your fonts.

Ligatures

I have been guilty in the recent past of adding dozens of ligatures to my fonts. I especially like ligatures for the gg and bb combinations. But there are many more:

sp, st, ch, gg, bb, Th, sk, ry, tt, ty, ffy, ct, Wh, just to show few.

What has been sad to me is that these fun additions to your copy are usually the first complaint I hear from typographically ignorant clients and readers. So, I've been forced to drop their use. What can I say?

The only two required by the normal 8-bit glyph choices are the fi and fl ligatures. Just remember, if "normal" people notice the ligatures—they'll complain.

Swashes et al

Quite often I want something special for the QQ or the KK or the RR or the AA. They do add hand spacing issues in most cases.

Adding the additional characters

Though it is quite complicated to add a lot of special characters and other languages, it is quite possible that you are adding these marks to a copy of a font you own. You like the font but it does not have some of the characters you need regularly. In that case you need to add the blank character slots needed.

To add characters

You start by opening Font Info. Click on the Encoding page tab and increase the number of glyphs available. When you click OK, the new blank character slots will be added at the end of the font. Then select the character you wish to specify, type Command+I to get the Selection Info dialog, and type in the Unicode number needed. You can start with the Unicode number by locating that code in the list of all Unicode characters found on Wikipedia. It will be listed as U+xxxx. All you need are the four characters after the plus. Type that in and click the Encoding button to get the name.

Adding Kcommaaccent

Glyph Information		
Glyph Name: Kcommaaccent	Get From: Unicode	Encoding
Unicode Codepoint: 0136	Get From: Name	
Unicode Name: LATIN CAPITAL LETTER K CEDILLA		
▶ Contour and fill properties (Type 3 fonts)		
	Cancel	OK

Here you can see I typed in Kcommaaccent. This is what the slot is named in fonts. When I clicked on the Name button next to Unicode Codepoint, the code 0136 was added. Underneath is the Unicode Name: LATIN CAPITAL LETTER K CEDILLA. What this all means I have no a clue. I didn't even know in which language it is used [it turns out to be Latvian]. Again, it works equally well to type in the 0136 and click the Encoding button.

OpenType features

It's tough! I don't want to have to say this, but Fontographer does not do OpenType well at all. In the template I made up for us to use for this font, I included 3-4 OpenType features. When I opened the font and resaved it, I attached the proper OpenType feature file to it in the Font Info Encoding page under OpenType Layout to make the glyph substitutions work. I had placed the smcapoldstyle.fea file that comes with the template into the features folder in application support in the users folder (Mac OSX). Here's the path for that: /Users/[username]/Library/Application Support/FontLab/Fontographer 5/Features/smcapoldstyle.fea

So, what's the problem?

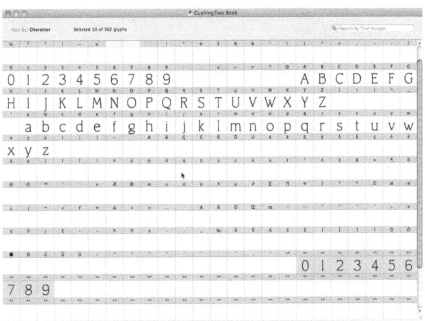

I can't see anything. If you look at the capture above, you can see I have added the numbers to the oldstyle figures slots. How do I know that? I can't see it. All I can do

is select the figures above and copy them. Then I find the zero.oldstyle slot and select to the right counting off the selection until I have all ten slots selected. Then I paste. The result is what you see below. The glyphs are in the right position, but Fontographer does not give us any indication of that, at all. All I can do is hope that Fontographer does it right. (It did. The features worked fine when I exported the font.)

If you look closely, you'll see that all the new glyphs have a character name of **. If I have Names added to the Info Bar at the top of Font Window, it will tell me the name of the glyph. It's not Fontographer's fault. Fontographer shows us the Unicode name. The problem is that there is no Unicode name for any of the features I added to the template. Neither oldstyle figures nor small caps (and especially not small cap figures) have Unicode names. They are not on the Unicode list. Unicode simply sees them as variant forms of the original character.

Designing oldstyle figures

You do not need to make these an OpenType feature. You can simply use them as your numbers in your normal 8-bit or OpenType Std font.

You can also call oldstyle figures lowercase numbers (but no one except an ignorant beginner would do that). They are designed to be used in normal text: sentence case. They blend in beautifully with the lowercase letters. They have the same x-height as the lowercase and the same ascender and descender measurements.

For all of my fonts, I have both oldstyle figures and proportional lining figures (I usually also include monospaced lining figures for the bookkeepers among my user base).

Let's run through them. The most normal setup uses 0, 1, and 2 at the x-height; 6 and 8 having ascenders; and 3, 4, 5, 7, and 9 having descenders. However, there are no real rules. For years I used 4 with a descender and I still like that best. An old French setup used an above line 3 up to the ascender. Again, you can find very strongly stated opinions on typophile. But, it's your font. Have fun!

It is important to keep the weights consistent with the rest of the characters. I'll share some of the assumed normals, but don't take them too seriously. Make your oldstyle figures work well with your lowercase type. That's all that matters.

Oldstyle zero 0 [X-HEIGHT]

This zero is a bit condensed, especially if the lowercase o is almost round. If the lowercase o is condensed, then the oldstyle zero should maybe be round. Make them different.

Oldstyle one 1

This is pretty obvious except for the fact that the top serif is usually flat. The sloped arm of the lining number one is raised to a horizontal.

Oldstyle two 2

This takes the most work of the oldstyle figures because of the same issues as we worked with in the lowercase a and e—three horizontals within the x-height.

Oldstyle three 3

Here the only issue is whether or not you want the center horizontal to fall on the baseline. Usually you can not do that without massive distortions because the x-height is taller than the descender.

Oldstyle four 4

Here the bottom of the top triangle definitely needs to fall on the baseline.

Oldstyle five 5

Here the center horizontal needs to be above the baseline or the 5 looks very strange.

Oldstyle six 6

No changes

Oldstyle seven 7

You normally need to shorten the stem.

Oldstyle eight 8

No changes

Oldstyle nine 9

This takes quite bit of work to shorten the lower arm after you rotate a copy of the six.

Other oldstyle glyphs /.,#$%¥£¢€

What others?

You need a whole set of companion glyphs to go with the oldstyle figures: /.,()$%¥£¢€—at least. [That's the way the feature file is written.] As you can see, I usually make my oldstyle $ the x-height and then move it up to the descender or cap height line. I do the same with the number symbol #. I make the ¥£¢€ the x-height tall. But these companion glyphs are an unusual quirk on my part which I use because I think it makes the oldstyle numbers read better.

Building the small caps

This is slightly tedious work. First you must select the caps A-Z and copy them. Then locate the small cap slots, and paste in copies of the Caps. Then reduce them down, to the x-height (usually). Finally you must adjust all the weight measurements so that they match the rest of the font. You must also do this for the 0-9 and paste them into the zero. sc to nine.sc slots (of course they must be lining numerals to do that). Again, small cap figures are an unusual quirk of mine that I find essential to use within small cap text. As far as I know no one else is using them—yet.

You need to do this quite carefully. What this means in actual workflow, is that you try things. If it doesn't work you undo and try again. Be prepared to do and redo several times as each font is different.

If your modifications do not work, you cannot undo from the Font window: You must open the A.sc or zero.sc and type Command+Z to undo. Then continue to hold the Command key down and type the right bracket to go to the next character, type Z, then], then Z and so on until you have them all redone. You may need to do this several times while you determine how much to scale and change weight.

Especially for bold fonts, it is very easy to plug the counters. Also the more extreme the changes, the more distortions you'll find in the paths. So, you want to make minimal changes. I find this more difficult than the original design of the letters. But then I do not do well with repetitive things like this. Part of that is that the design is already set—so a lot of the fun is gone. But keep at it. You should be able to get the bulk changes down in about four or five tries.

First I transform

I divide the x-height by the cap height. For CushingTwo that gives me 72%. So, I Scale Uniformly 72%.

Then I change weight

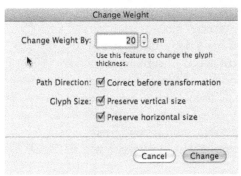

Because the numbers and letters are scaled down, the weight is scaled also. So, we need to make the small caps a little bolder after they are scaled. I tried several things here. I ended up set up like you see—but set at 15 ems. This fattened up the minimum to its proper weight without over-fattening all the others. Now I need to go through all 26 small caps and the ten figures to adjust the weights. Remember what you use because you will be using the settings for several other characters as we go through this process (like the small cap æ, ð, ı, and so on).

As I get started, I notice my first problem. The serifs were fattened up also. They are 3 emus thicker. So, I drag in guides to indicate the height of the serifs before they were transformed. However, the guides are mainly to remind me. In most cases, all I have to do is select the errant points and move them up or down 3 emus. That amount does not distort the lettershapes too much—it's normally not noticeable.

Check the overshoots

I'm finding that the overshoots are also scaled so I am having to move the top up 3 emus and the bottom down 3 emus if there is any overshoot involved. The letters without overshoots seem to fit exactly.

Much better than FontLab

What I am finding is that the change weight function is much better with far less distortion than I have to deal with in FontLab. Increasingly I can see that I will be doing my drawing and spacing here in Fontographer and going to FontLab for the OpenType feature development. That remains to be seen. Fontographer is winning me over.

 Neat trick for cut/paste: This may not affect you, but I just had a nice thing happen. One of the problems with FontLab is that cutting the content from a character slot, deletes the slot. In Fontographer if you have a character in the wrong slot you can simply cut it and paste it into the correct slot—in the Font window. I no longer have to open the outline window to do that. Plus, in the case just cited, my small cap zero-nine was one slot to the right. I selected all ten, cut them, and pasted them into the correct slots. I suspect you assumed that. But I thought I'd mention it.

What I am doing now (and have been doing for the past 3-4 hours) is checking weights and assembling composites. The small caps need the same accented characters as the caps. After four hours, it looks like what you see on the next page. As you can see it goes pretty quick:

I know you can't really see anything, but I wanted you to see that once things get going, much of the work is built from pieces you have already developed. So, it goes pretty quickly at this point. For this font we are talking about 371 characters and as you can see we are well over half done.

The key is finding patterns to paste and making sure you use the Command+G (Get component) instead of Command+C (Copy). I paste in the vowels first to set the letterspacing. Then I add the accents. You should know that you can do it by holding down the command key and then type v to paste and] to move to the next slot. Like I said look for patterns. Paste all the As, then all the Es, and so on. For a glyph like the Œ, paste in the O component, then open the Outline window, paste in the E. Move the components until they overlap properly, decompose, and remove the overlap. It goes very quickly.

The special characters

Until you have your own style built up for these characters, this will take a while. You can certainly use the ones I provided in the template, but it takes some time to learn what works, what looks good as far as you are concerned, and to develop good work habits.

Adding your own dingbats

If you are making a font for your own use, do not hesitate to add your own dingbats in the slots of the special characters you never use. As I mentioned, I always put an open ballot box in the Section slot [Option+6—□]. I have never used a section character. If I found I needed one, I guess I'd know I was hanging around the wrong crowd. ;-)

This is supposed to be fun, remember?

It's now a week later. At about an hour a day or so, I gradually assembled all the pieces for the OpenType features. Yes, it is tedious work. But, if you take it a little bit at a time it goes pretty quickly.

Finishing the letterspacing

Letterspacing has been a real fight for me while writing this book, as I am used to spending quite a bit of time hand spacing each letter as I draw it. Trusting the auto-spacing has been rough for me. But it is working well. I need to remember that I did without careful hand spacing for the first decade of my font design career.

My goal, so far, has been to show you how to put a font together for the fun of it. It has been enjoyable to get back to actual font design without all the work of careful hand letterspacing.

Benefits of auto spacing

The advantages of working without worrying about the spacing are something I need to consider as I move on in my design career. Selling the fonts will still require the type of hand spacing I cover in Appendix A. However, the freedom I've enjoyed so far seems to help the designs.

I finally finished the rough shapes this morning. I ran the Auto Space set at 65—it took 120 seconds. There were no real issues. Then I selected all the small cap numbers, letters and composites and spaced them a little wider at 75.

Auto Kern settings

Then I ran the Auto Kern. This took a bit longer. I left the settings for spacing at the same as I used for the letterspacing. But there were a couple of changes I made in the advanced choices of the Auto Kern dialog box. We need to go through these like we did for Auto Space.

Advanced Auto Kern Settings

Here we have four pages. Let's go through them and talk a little about the options.

Kerning settings

Here the key is to use the same number you used for Auto Space. As far as number of kerning pairs is concerned, I've had to change my mind. I've always done as many as necessary, but I recently discovered that this made the Web font versions too large. The problem is that there is no way to remove an excessive number of kerning pairs in Fontographer. You need to go to FontLab to remove them. So, I suggest you limit them to 1500 pairs. However, the unlimited fonts really looked good in print—even though sixteen thousand kerning pairs are clearly ridiculous.

So maybe two versions will be necessary. It depends on how and where you use them. If you want to use them online with @fontface in a Website, then you might well want to restrict your font to 500 pairs or less. Few browsers support kerning at this time anyway. But that will probably change as online type gets better. It will really ramp up when ePUBs can take embedded fonts.

It is easy enough to make a new font for the Web before you do the spacing for print. Then copy/paste the glyphs into the new font and space it for the online limitations. I'll just mention the need to convert your OpenType fonts to 8-bit (256 character) versions on the Web because there is no online support for OpenType—except in FireFox, so far (fall 2011). Even there it is limited. But full support is part of the CSS3 spec—so it's coming.

Glyphs settings

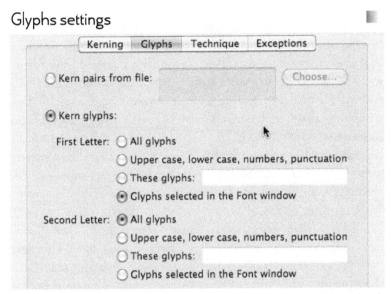

I set it to kern ALL glyphs to start. I remember back in the late 1990s, that I used to crash Fontographer all the time when I did this. But then, as I recall, I only had 128 MB RAM and maybe only 64 MB. Now I have an iMac with Snow Leopard and 4 GB RAM. That certainly helps.

Exceptions settings

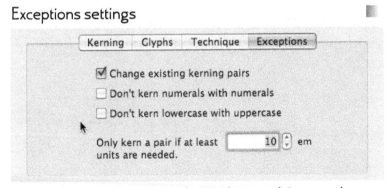

I do want kerning with numbers and I certainly want kerns between lowercase and uppercase. I need this for doing URLs if nothing else. Modern Web addresses and software names have caps and numbers scattered throughout the words we now use. So, I unchecked two of the boxes on the Exceptions page.

Plus, I changed minimum kerning point to 10 em. The minimum was 20 ems. Moving that figure to 10 ems ensures that everything that should be kerned was kerned. The result was that I ended up with almost 15500 kerning pairs. This sounds absolutely horrible to font design traditionalists. But we are dealing with 371 characters. With many OpenType fonts this number is quite small. If you start including all the eastern European glyphs , and the Greek, plus numerators, denominators, discretionary ligatures, and swashes, the character count can easily rise to 1000 characters or more. For example, Caflisch Script has 1343. Zapfino has 1503.

Plus, with my FontLab fonts I always had glyphs from my OpenType features that were never spaced right. I wanted it all spaced well. It is. I am very pleased with the results of the spacing. The font seems to work really well right out of the chute. I did have some issues, though. Not with Fontographer's spacing but with my glyph designs.

Technique settings

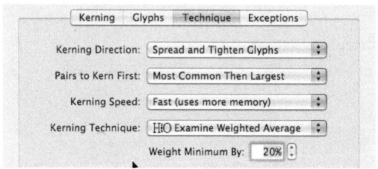

Remember the weight minimum is set at the same figure as it is on the Technique page of Auto Space.

Dealing with the small caps

As I mentioned briefly before we started kerning, the small caps need to be spaced more than the lowercase. For

CushingTwo I selected all the small caps, including the numbers and auto spaced them at 75 instead of 65 (like I did all the rest). This seemed to help.

I did the same thing with the auto kerning. I selected all the small caps and changed the auto kerning for those small caps in both the first letter and the second letter to "Glyphs selected in the Font window".

 The excessive kerning: This seems to be a solution for the relatively crude letterspacing created by auto spacing. It's not the best thing, but it works fine. If you are going to sell the fonts, on the other hand, you really need to read Appendix A and start hand spacing your fonts. It's not that painful, and the fonts really do look a lot better in the applications like InDesign which support good metrics and kerning.

I'll continue to do more testing. When I find things, I'll post them in The Skilled Workman blog. I expect to abandon my typography blog on Blogger simply because the blogging interface is so inadequate there.

Finishing the font

Fixing the rough glyphs

Now we begin to see why I call these rough glyphs at this point. As I looked at the printed proof using some sample text I keep around, I started noticing issues. The first thing I noticed was that the e looked a little dark on the sides. When I went back into Fontographer to check it out, I discovered that I had never checked the width of the stroke at the extrema of the bowls horizontally.

As I recall, now, I started checking that while I was doing the small caps. Now I started going through the font and I found that the right and left extrema of the bowls were all too wide with very few exceptions.

Because of the ll glyph with the pieces this was very easy to adjust and repair. It took only about 5 minutes to adjust the entire font. The good news is that fixing the e also fixed all the composite "e"s.

As I went through the font with my eyes opened to the new problem. I saw little things on virtually all the glyphs with curves. However, because I had been careful putting things together, all of these changes [and I changed about 25 out of the 62 basic glyphs] took less than 15 minutes.

Rechecking the font

Each time I made adjustments, I regenerated the fonts in both .otf and .ttf. I'd then delete the font out of my font management software and reinstall the newer version. Then I printed out another copy of the test page.

I'm now convinced that what I have is good enough to move on. What I need to do next is make a bold version. On the next page let me show you what the font looks like now.

AaBbCcDdEeFfGg
HhIiJjKkLlMmNnOo
PpQqRrSsTtUuVv
WwXxYyZz&$@*?!
1234567890¢€¥$
1234567890¢€¥$
1234567890¢€¥$ABCD
EFGHIJKLMNOPQRSTU
vwxyzŁΩæÐffl¾...

Doing a bold version

Now we need to make a bold version. Here again, we will make Fontographer do the heavy lifting. As I am regaining confidence in the software, I am certain that we can greatly shorten the design time with no real problem.

Change the weight

I decided to change the weight by 27 ems using the Change Weight... dialog box—can't give you a good reason. Once I did that I quickly look over the resultant changed glyphs. The r is all greyed out and weird. So I open the outline window for that r. Here's what I find.

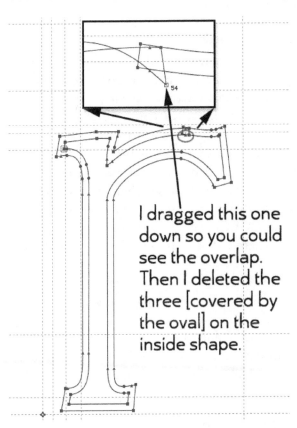

I dragged this one down so you could see the overlap. Then I deleted the three [covered by the oval] on the inside shape.

For some reason, the r has developed an interior path running around in the opposite direction that was not deleted.

How did this happen?

I'm sure some geek could tell me, but I really don't care. I can fix it in less than a minute. I delete the three interior points seen in the capture. I double-click the interior path and delete it. And then I drag the endpoint on the remaining path on top of the other endpoint and merge. I actually did it quite a bit more quickly than it has taken to write the procedure out for you.

Don't get uptight about these things.
Just fix them.

The overall result is fantastic!

I am very pleased. When I used to do these things in Fontographer 4, and when I do them in FontLab, I usually get many bad glyphs the first time. In fact, if you've read my *Practical Font Design* book for FontLab, you'll see that I recommend making things bold with only the basic 62 glyphs finished. This solved some of the problems. But I like living dangerously. So, I did it all at one whack.

What a joyful surprise! Fontographer did an excellent job. As I look through it very quickly, I'm expecting to fix it all in a few hours. Of course there are many small issues. I'll share some of them as I go through the font—beginning with the cap A.

Right off, I get good news. When I changed the weight on all the glyphs, it made the weight balls bold also. It really messed up the open paths I used for the serifs—but I can just delete them. I don't need them any more. When I place the ll component into the cap A outline window, I find that the weight balls are the right size and they fit the transformed glyph.

What a timesaver this is!

Deciding about the serifs

As I'm sure you thought about, yes, the serifs got bold also. Now I must decide what to do about that. What you are going to find is that many tiny things like this are not quite what you need them to be.

For example, I want to change the guides to reflect the new thicker serifs. More than that I want to look at them very carefully. I have found over the years that the serifs are what get chewed up the most when changing the weight of a font. You need to look them over very carefully. In fact, you need to check every path on every glyph very carefully. Even if we do not have to redraw most of them (and that looks to be the case), we'll still need to do very careful adjustments to get things right.

On the A the serifs do not look too bad. I check out the entire glyph with the weight balls. But then I decide to check out the lowercase u. I am fixing the guides to match up with the new thickness of the serifs and I need to adjust the guide for the x-height also. When I open the u to do the same thing, this is what I see.

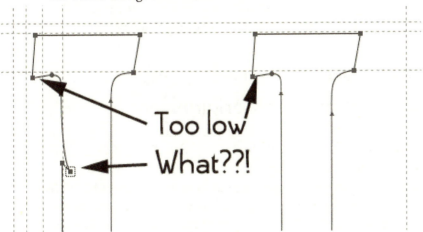

Here you can see clearly the type of things you will need to fix. The tops of the top serifs are 2 emus too low. The left bottom corners of the serifs are 4 or 5 emus too low. And look what the bolding process did to the left side of the left stem. That little notch is typical of the issues you will discover. Some judicious merging and slight moving and adjusting to the points and handles fix all these issues very quickly [much more quickly than I could write about them]. Basically, you need to train your eye to see the problems.

Extraneous points: One of the things that has happened is that extra points have been added on most of the paths. They only make the font more complex, and they rarely help the actual shape. Get rid of all the ones you can by Merging them away. If the shape changes too much, simply undo and leave that one alone.

Sometimes, especially on straight line sections, you can marquee/merge several points at once. Other times, you'll need to carefully do them one at a time. Often, you'll need to try one. Undo, try another. Undo. And so on until you get the path massaged into shape. The good news is that you get very fast at this very quickly.

An important thing to remember is to Clean Up the paths [Command+Shift+C] to add the extrema if you mess them up. For these operations I usually turn off the Simplify Paths checkbox. It merely adds more points to delete—in most cases.

This is where you find out how well you drew the original font

If you did a good clean job of drawing the original shapes, your repairs on the bold version will be clean, simple, and easy to fix. If you left a lot of extra points and bad curves [without extrema] in your original font, you'll have a horrible job ahead of you. The extrema are used to determine the bounding box. This sets the size of the transformations and the general shapes.

In many cases, as you first begin this part of your font design learning process, you will find it is much quicker and more simple to go back to original and fix the paths there.

Then start over with the bolding process. Once you get the idea of how to put paths together, it is almost always much quicker to fix the results.

Things will vary a lot

I just went through EFGHIJ with almost no changes. Then K had a bunch—just little things, but several of them. It's actually going very fast. It's been about two hours of hard labor this morning, but the bold version is almost finished. As usual, the problem glyphs were the Ks, 4s, and pieces like the @.

Also as normal, the serifs are a little chewed up. Sometimes it may be good to redesign the serifs and replace them all. But that's not very difficult either. All in all, it is going much faster than it does in FontLab. I'm pleased.

I just finished it; generated fonts; and proofed it. There's only one problem. It's not really bold. It's more like a really nice Medium. Changing weight by 27 ems is more like an incremental step to medium. I do not want to take up more of your time here by doing an actual bold, and then an extra bold. But you will need to deal with this.

Dealing with the different weights

But I must talk about it. It's the old naming thing which is controlled by Windows. What do I mean by that? Now we're delving into a snarl within the font design world. Much of font design is controlled by Windows folks. What I mean is that Windows invented a fictional position that fonts always come in families: regular, italic, bold, and bold italic. Now, if you've been around fonts for any time at all you know that this simply is not true and has never been true except in the lalaland of the PC. It's not really even true there. HOWEVER!

If you do not design your families in the four-font mode: RIBBI, your PC customers will start complaining and you'll have to fix the problem by renaming everything. You may have noticed with some of my font families I have a [family] Book version with Book, Book Italic, Book Bold, and Book Bold Italic. And I have a [family] version that is RIBBI—but it should actually be named Medium, Medium Italic, Black, and Black Italic.

Fontographer buys into this because it is necessary. When I made my CushingTwo Medium font (and clicked the build names button in Font Info), it installed as a separate font

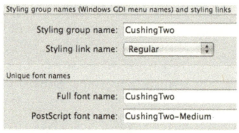

family. This happened because clicking on Build Names changed the Styling group name: to CushingTwo Med. So, I changed it back to CushingTwo, as you see above.

So, problem solved, right? Yup, on a Mac—apparently (but not for long). The problem is the drop down menu which is labeled "Styling link name". It only lists four styling links: Regular, Italic, Bold, and Bold italic. So, you only have those four options with any styling group name.

Here's what happened down the road: I went on to make my bold font. By changing the styling group name, I ended up with CushingTwo Book, CushingTwo Medium,and CushingTwo Bold. When I installed them, they grouped into a family and the three choices appeared in my font listings in my applications with no issues.

When I made my Obliques, everything went fine until I came to CushingTwo Medium Italic. I'd already used Regular for Book and Bold for Bold. So, Book Italic became Regular Italic. Bold Italic was fine (although if I had named the font CushingTwo Heavy the Windows people would still see CushingTwo Bold Italic). CushingTwo Medium had no place to fit within this scenario.

So finally I made the middle weight demibold. I changed the styling group name to CushingTwo Demi. Because it is a different styling group, it shows up separately in the font lists. But it works everywhere: Mac or PC. It's not elegant, but there is no option presently.

The problem is the slope

As soon as I change the slope to Italic or Oblique [the other options are Cursive, Kursiv, Inclined, Sloped, and Slanted], I've entered the wild world of nonprofessional page layout software. OK, it's the normal world for those of you who actually work with Office and even lesser software. I'm fortunate in that I do all my work within the Creative Suite (about 90% within InDesign). In my world, I select the actual fonts I need to use.

In that so-called normal world where others live, it is expected that if they install a font like CushingTwo Demi, they can type Ctrl+I and get CushingTwo Demi Italic. It is quite possible that, after I upload my 6-font CushingTwo family, MyFonts or one of the Monotype sites will get a complaining whine that when they type Ctrl+B when using CushingTwo Demi, they do not get a bold.

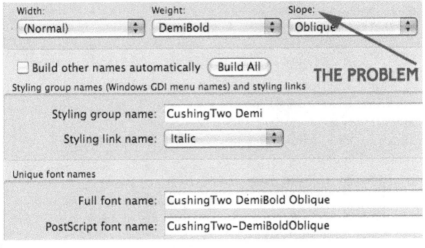

I could force the issue

It is certainly possible for me to set my fonts up so they are all grouped in the same family in the font menu. If I do this, CushingTwo Demibold will not have an italic style to choose. In this scenario, CushingTwo Demibold Italic will show up as one of my font names, but the styling link name will be regular. Mass chaos will reign and the font police will be knocking at my door. Such confusion is anathema. So, don't do it!

Font Information						
		Mode:	○ Easy	⊙ Advanced		

Names	Dimensions	Encoding	Credits	Licensing	Recommendations

Typographic names (Mac and OpenType menu names)

Typographic family name: CushingTwo
Should be identical across the typographic family

Typographic style name: Demi Italic ☐ Auto
Must be unique within the typographic family

Design parameters

Width: (Normal) Weight: DemiBold Slope: (Plain) Other:

☐ Build other names automatically (Build All)
Styling group names (Windows GDI menu names) and styling links

Styling group name: CushingTwo

Styling link name: Regular

Unique font names

Full font name: CushingTwo DemiBold Italic

PostScript font name: CushingTwo-DemiBoldItalic

Your only real choice is go along with the world as it is (I know, what a drag), and set up a second styling group name. If you go over eight styles, or if you want to make a condensed or expanded version, you will need to add still more styling groups.

 Unlimited regulars: To rephrase all of this. When you are designing a font family of weights and styles, you can have as many fonts with Regular styling link names as you like. But you can only have one Italic, one Bold, and one Bold Italic styling link. Those three will be applied with the Command+B and Command+I shortcuts in Office.

I did design a bold version

The problems multiplied—as expected—when I fattened it another 27 ems. The serifs were now so distorted that I basically had to start over. I needed to decide how much to narrow the vertical serifs—like the ones on the end of the crossbar of the E & F. I had to make new serif pieces and the whole nine yards.

However, because I had it all worked out conceptually the actual production went very fast. Of course, part of it is that I am now back in the Fontographer mode again after nearly a decade working in FontLab. Fontographer works really fast once you master the paradigm of the app.

As usual, my ll slot is filling up

I just started out with the three weight balls I knew I would need—adding a border to keep them clearly visible as I moved them around for resizing the stroke weights. Then I added the three serif pieces, as I normally do. Then it became obvious that I needed an arm piece. Bolding the second time like this had really chewed up the serifs. So I needed the consistency provided by these pieces.

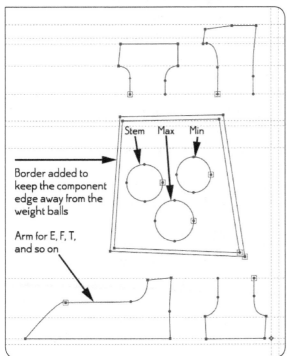

Stem Max Min

Border added to keep the component edge away from the weight balls

Arm for E, F, T, and so on

This type of thing happens for every design, and it is different each time. That is why I developed the ll slot, putting it as the last slot for easy access and selection.

It was too difficult to find endpoints I could merge for the arm piece. There were going to be no neat endpoints with which to join. So, I made the arm a closed shape by simply merging all the unneeded points in the E. This closed shape I could move into position easily and then use Remove Overlap.

Plugging counters: By this time glyphs like the ©, ®, ℗, #, $, and most of the small caps were filling in. As the glyphs remained the same height and width, the expanding stroke width encroached the counters from all sides. It took some careful, and creative adjustments.

Adding an italic

Now that I had three fonts: Book, Medium, and Bold, it was hard to avoid the need for italics or at least obliques. One scenario for this is very fast. It is the one I used for CushingTwo. In the font window, I can select all, type Command+\ (to get transform), slant it a bit (-7° To -11° usually), and do a "modern" italic. Why we use minus (or negative) degree numbers I do not know, nor does it really matter. The results are very quick.

When I have everything slanted, I run Auto Space and Auto Kern again. Then I go through all the composited glyphs and realign all the accents. I've not found a good way to move the accents with the characters. Of course, I could Select All and Decompose. Then the accents would move with the characters (like the dots do with the i and j). But I don't like to do that. I may well find that one of my accents is ugly or worse. I want to be able to fix that and have it changed throughout the font. The choice is yours.

Technically this new font is an Oblique. I usually make a few changes like changing the a and g from two-story to one story and a few changes like that. How far you want to go with that is up to you.

A true italic is a whole other story—as you well know. As I do not really like italics, I'm not the man to talk about that for you. However, the principles are the same.

Adding slanted guides

If you are actually drawing true italics, you'll certainly need some slanted guides. You can draw them on the guides layer with the line tool. Another place you might want to do this is in the ll spot with your weight balls. You might need to add a slanted piece to help you maintain the look. Again you simply produce the pieces you need to get the job done efficiently. For CushingTwo I didn't bother. A fancy italic seems out of character with the look.

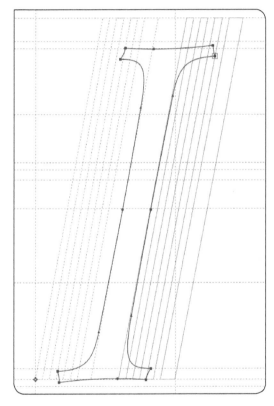

Here's a set of hand spacing guides I set up for a current font

You'll need to read Appendix A to see what I am doing here and why. It works quite easily.

In CushingTwo, as a result of my choices, I was able to make, and generate oblique fonts for all three of my new fonts in about an hour. I now have a new six font family. CushingTwo has Book, Bold, Book Italic, and Bold Italic. CushingTwo Demi has Regular and Italic. Over the next week or so, I'll test out the fonts by using them. I will then get them uploaded for sale.

Regardless, I'm pleased & I had fun drawing them. That's what matters to me.

Generating a font

The manual has good and complete instructions. It has the
best explanation of the various font formats that I've seen.
Basically you enter here into an area you do not want to deal
with. My advice for Fontographer is to use the easy method
and generate cross-platform fonts in an .otf and a .ttf version

This is a refresher image of the dialog box opened by
typing the Command+Option+G command. If you have an
OpenType feature file (as we do for CushingTwo) and it is
linked in the File Info dialog box, Fontographer will use it
to compile your OpenType fonts.

Web fonts

As you saw when we were discussing layers, I do not
deal with hinting. I spent a lot of time while writing this
book with Richard Fink, producer of the Readable Web blog
and one of the emerging experts on the issues surrounding Web fonts. He contacted many of his friends, like Mark
Simonson, Thomas Phinney and others. What we found was
no clear consensus. The problem is in the Windows world
where hinting of TrueType fonts is required.

In addition, Web fonts are all still 8-bit (256 character fonts). My current solution is to save a version of my
OpenType font to use for pieces to build my Web fonts. I
currently produce an Oldstyle version with oldstyle figures,
a Smallcaps version with lining figures and small caps, and
a limited small cap figures version. I generate them as True-
Type with auto hinting turned on. Other than that I do not
use hinting. Contact Richard if you decide to go a different
way for your Web fonts. Even Richard calls hinting TrueType
voodoo. Very few take the time to do it well.

As I find out better methods, I'll post them on my blog,
The Skilled Workman.

Other formats

If you feel compelled to really get into font format gen-
eration (producing Type 1 and TrueType fonts for the Mac and
another set for the PC), that is far beyond the scope of this
book and you need to study the manual and work until you
get something that satisfies your need. If you are intrigued
by Multiple Master fonts, get over it. You may be able to use
it for some of your internal production issues, but Adobe
has dropped support for MM fonts—as has everyone else.

Beginning a new font of your own

Italia Book

ABCDEFGHIJ
KLMNOPQR
STUVWXYZ
1234567890

abcdefghijkl
mnopqrstuv
wxyz

This font is also designed by Colin Brignall in 1977 for Letraset, MyFonts gives it this history: 1890, William Morris, Golden Type, Kelmscott Press; to 1893, Joseph W. Phinney, Jenson Oldstyle, Dickinson Type Foundry (American Type Founders), which was based on Morris' Golden Type. Both were modeled on the mid-1400s letters of Nicolas Jenson; to 1977, Colin Brignall redrew the ATF Jenson series for Letraset, and renamed the design Italia.

Before we can talk about new font designs, we need to cover the standard terminology used to describe font styles. Of course that again assumes that there is a standard. As with most things typographic, there are many standards. In fact, there are probably nearly as many standards as there are fonts designers—a couple thousand or so. But we can come to some general agreement.

In addition, we need to review what has happened over the past half millennium to get our minds and eyes trained to see the little variations we are dealing with in new font designs. My goal is to teach you to consciously deal with all of these design issues to help improve your designs.

Type Classifications

Let's begin by talking a bit about classifying the stunningly rapid increase in the number of fonts with which we must deal today. In the 19th century there were barely hundreds of designs. By the mid-20th century, there were several hundred. By the 1990s, there were a couple thousand different fonts. By now, there are hundreds of thousands of fonts. Many of the really interesting ones are free fonts.

As mentioned, the problem (if you want to call it that) is that there really are no standards—or the standards are still related to letterpress designs that are centuries old. This problem has gotten worse because most of the new design-ers come from outside the font industry. Font design is the Wild West, with everyone doing what is right in their own eyes, according their own opinions.

Various systems & making sense of the mess

The snarl you saw in the history description of Italia on the preceding page, where a font design is traced through its roots, is typical of what we deal with in font design. As I have mentioned, there is no way for me to strip out the influence of Colin and Letraset to my design style. But, according to MyFonts, Italia came from Jenson via Morris and Phinney. Italia is considered a radical new style but as you can see everything is stolen from earlier sources. That is the nature of this design field.

We apply our sense of style and taste to existing designs. Everyone defends their turf vigorously, but really it's all so inbred that you can hardly pick out who sourced who. We may get into the legalities later. But you know what plagiarism is. Don't do it.

A practical approach to classifying fonts

There are many of these classification systems. Robert Bringhurst, in the currently accepted standard reference on typography, *The Elements of Typographic Style*, Hartley and Marks, 1992, uses historical markers. He sets up categories based largely on historical periods of fine art as you can see in the sidebar on the next page. It is, indeed, a fascinat-ing journey through art history. Robert presents his case extremely well. He's an excellent writer and a poet. You will acquire a great deal of useful knowledge by reading his book.

It is a bit over the top, though. Plus, he skips a lot. Bringhurst clearly does not like Victorian letter styles, so he does not mention them. He skips all of the modern variations like Art Nouveau, Art Deco, and the more extreme elements of the early twentieth century. He barely mentions the slab serifs of the late nineteenth century because he thinks they are coarse. On the other hand, he has several categories for that stiff, cold, distant class of styles called modern (which he obviously likes a great deal). In other words, he presents the type he likes in an excellent setting.

Bringhurst's List

Scribal or Carolingian

Renaissance

Mannerist

Baroque

Rococo

Neoclassical

Romantic

Realist

Geometric Modernism

Expressionist

Elegiac Post-Modernism

Geometric Post-Modernism.

One of the more entertaining resources on the Web is Jonathan Hoefler's *Typography 101* writings on typophile.com. Like Bringhurst, his classes make a lot of sense and we'll include them in our practical list as we go through. He starts with two that are fun. They really have no place in a general classification system other than the fact that they show the historical roots of type in European culture. Remember, the study of type is a European thing.

Lithos

ABCDEFGHIJ
KLMNOPQR
STUVWXYZ
1234567890
ABCDEFGHIJK
LMNOPQRST
UVWXYZ

Lapidary:

He distinguishes Greek Inscriptions from Roman. Basically, the Greeks did not use serifs. He uses Lithos by Carol Twombley from Adobe in 1989 as his standard here. It was the fashion standard of the period. Like all fashion statements, it seems pretty dated now. But it is still a pretty design though the lack of a lowercase hurts.

Inscriptional:

Here's the Roman variant. Hoefler uses Twombly at Adobe again with her font called Trajan, from the Trajan column in Rome.

Again, it is a beautiful font but limited in usage. While historically accurate, the lack of a lowercase really limits the use.

These two styles are fun, but not too important to an overall classification system, because there are so few of these fonts. The rest of Hoefler's classes we'll cover in the practical list that follows.

Trajan
ABCDEFGHIJ
KLMNOPQR
STUVWXYZ
1234567890
ABCDEFGHIJK
LMNOPQRST
UVWXYZ

Thomas Phinney, now gone from Adobe, wrote a nice little historical piece (it seems to have been pulled off the Web). In it, he uses the more common set of categories currently taught in most design schools: Old Style, Transitional, Modern, Slab Serif (or Egyptian), fat faces, wood type, Art Nouveau, Art Deco, synthesis, and grunge. This covers the basics nicely and we will roughly follow that "normal" lead. However, let's get real.

The important thing isn't historical accuracy, it is readability and decorative style.

The importance of classification has to do with appropriateness. Bringhurst is still over the top here when he suggests using French type for French products and so on. However, you cannot pull off a Western "Wanted" poster with anything but Victorian type from the late 1880s. All of the recent Retro looks have specifically used fonts from a historical period placed in a hip, fashionable setting. Within a few months there were Retro fonts specifically designed to match the style. At this point in graphic design, the fonts appear along with the new fashion.

A practical list

The four basic classifications of all type are:

Serif   Script

Sans Serif   Decorative

Of course, most of the so-called Decorative fonts are serif or sans. Miscellaneous would be a better term. We'll start with the majority: serif typefaces. Serif fonts have been the dominant standard for typography for 500 years.

Only with the new millennium have we seen a genuine movement away from serifs toward readable sans. This basic classification is broken up into sub classes that are bewildering in their complexity. But the general consensus is as follows.

Minimal Serif Font Classifications

Oldstyle	Modern
Transitional	**Slab**

Oldstyle fonts: readable and beautiful (1500-1750 or so)

For practical purposes, I include all fonts designed before the mid-eighteenth century in oldstyle. That's how everyone reads them except for typographers. We need to remember that our readers feel this way. The distinctions are only interesting to type designers & type nerds. But then this is a book for us, isn't it?

The original fonts used by Gutenberg were in blackletter, what is commonly referred to as Gothic or Old English by most. This has had its own development and we will include it if I decide to have a discussion of handwriting fonts or scripts after we cover serif and sans serif.

The fonts we are most comfortable reading are those based on character forms from the fifteenth to the eighteenth centuries. They include both Oldstyle and Transitional styles. I include most of the font designs developed for early printers. These start with the earliest fonts from the Renaissance. Remember printing triggered the Renaissance.

This type of font is the standard to which all other fonts are compared. They are full of smooth sensuous curves. They are light, and open — beautiful, comfortable, and elegant. The stems are vertical. The bowls are nearly circular. The crossbars often rise to the right (but usually only with the e). The axis is mostly humanist until the end of the period in the mid-1700s. The aperture is comfortably open. There is enough contrast to help but not enough to dominate. They are very easy to read.

Humanist axis: All of the basic Oldstyle category uses a slanted axis roughly derived from the angle in which the pen was held for calligraphy. In other words, the angle used by humans to write. This axis varies in degrees but is always slanted from upper left to lower right— the basic right-handed bigotry that forms many of the assumptions about type design. But then I'm a little subjective on this topic being sinister myself (a lefty). This is opposed to the Rational axis (vertical axis) found in Modern fonts around the beginning of the 19th century.

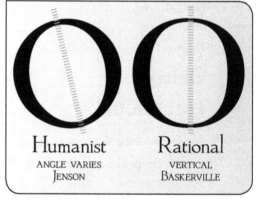

Humanist
ANGLE VARIES
JENSON

Rational
VERTICAL
BASKERVILLE

Venetian: Adobe Jenson Pro

Shortly after Gutenberg got things rolling in Germany a group of printers in Italy became interested in reviving some of the letterforms instituted by Charlemagne at the founding of the Holy Roman Empire in the 8th century.

The creative innovation was provided by Nicholas Jenson in Venice who combined the inscriptional caps with the Carolingian miniscules without many of the cursive remains. The gorgeous result is what we now call caps and lowercase (more properly upper and lower case), our basic assumed 52-character Latin alphabet.

Venetian characteristics

❦ **Wide caps:** The circular characters like the O are actually a circle drawn with a humanist axis.

❦ **Little modulation:** Often, there is little thick–thin contrast so the modulation is not readily apparent. However, that modulation is obvious in Jenson as you can see to the right.

> Adobe Jenson Pro
>
> ABCDEFGHIJ
> KLMNOPQR
> STUVWXYZ
> 1234567890
> abcdefghijklmn
> opqrstuvwxyz
>
> Robert Slimbach of Adobe used Nicolas Jenson's roman and Ludovico degli Arrighi's italic typeface designs as part of this family in the Adobe Originals historical revivals. *Adobe*

❦ **Slanted e:** The crossbar on the e is slanted and there is usually a little spur at the end of it.

❦ **Small counter in the a:** Look at how tiny it is in the sidebar above.

❦ **Slightly flared stems:** These flares are usually very subtle and unnoticed by readers.

- 🐦 Slightly inclined serifs: Usually showing their calligraphic roots by dipping a little on the left and trailing slightly wider on the right side.

& iduſtria **The original mess:** Scan of the original Jenson

In the original, there were many curious shapes. The neat, crisp digital shapes we are accustomed to today did not exist in the lead characters cast from hand carved metal molds. The scan in the subhead above is from the University of Florida's Rare Book collection.

www.uflib.ufl.edu/spec/rarebook/art3283c/15th.htm

Aldine: Bembo

These fonts are also from Northern Italy. Bembo is a revival of the work of another printer, Aldus Manutius in the 1500s. Manutius was a major influence on type design as we know it. Font style is coming under the control of the font designer (or punchcutter as they were known in the day). This continued the trend toward a more intellectual development of type away from its calligraphic roots.

Bembo

ABCDEFGHIJ
KLMNOPQR
STUVWXYZ
1234567890
abcdefghijklmn
opqrstuvwxyz

Aldine characteristics

- 🐦 Narrower caps: However, you can see that Bembo's OCQ are still round—actually they are slightly expanded.

- 🐦 Larger x-height: Although Slimbach's Jenson Pro had larger x-heights already in keeping with the fashion for large x-heights in the 1980s and 1990s.

- 🐦 Ascenders taller than the caps: This is the first case where this feature became a standard part of our font design lexicon. The caps are now usually 4% smaller than the ascenders—approximately.

❦ The horizontal line: Whereas the Venetian styles used the inclined line, the Aldine used the horizontal.

❦ Rigidly parallel stems: However, you can see the stems on Bembo's M are slanted.

❦ More regular serifs: Horizontal and symmetrical.

❦ Sheared apexes: AMNVW

Most of the life and playfulness of the Venetian has been ironed out. The term stately is used of these fonts—cool, formal, and sober. The English used these fonts as a base for what they called Old Face.

Garalde: Garamond 3

Garamond 3

ABCDEFGHIJ
KLMNOPQR
STUVWXYZ
1234567890
abcdefghijklmn
opqrstuvwxyz

This Linotype version of Garamond from 1936 is based on the American Type Founders design by Morris Fuller Benton and Thomas Maitland Cleland, who based their work, in turn, on seventeenth-century copies of Claude Garamond's types by Jean Jannon. *MyFonts*

The term comes from the combination of **Gara**mond and **Aldine**. These original serif fonts are exemplified by the work of Claude Garamond in Paris in the early to mid-1500s. Robert Slimbach released a new interpretation of Claude Garamond's and Robert Granjon's styles called Adobe Garamond Pro. Garamond was the first major type designer. He was not a printer nor a calligrapher, he was a freelance punchcutter. Along with Robert Granjon, Geofroy Tory, and others, they were responsible for what is now called the golden age of typography.

Some call this the French Aldine because this is a definite progression from those stately reserved fonts. Garamond lowered the x-height, and increased the height of the ascenders up and the height of the descenders down. The result was a classic font design that became the standard in Europe for the next 150 years. Writers wax rhapsodic about the majestic airiness & the like. I find it a bit boring—probably from overuse.

One of Claude's major innovations was the conscious decision to design a complementary italic companion font. As font design began, italics were completely separate. The first italic font cut was by Griffo, commissioned by Aldus Manutius again, in 1499. These early italics seem very condensed to us, with elliptical bowls and very calligraphic stroke endings (as opposed to actual serifs). Oddly, many of these italic fonts have vertical capital letters. This was the cursive handwriting of the period. They do not make good companions to modern fonts. They were closer to what we now call script.

Therefore they say unto God,

This is a capture of P22's Operina Romano taken from Ludovico Arrighi's 1522 instructional lettering book. Like all scans of the very early type examples, it looks really rough to our eyes. Below is Benton/Cleland's interpretation:

Garamond 3 Therefore they say
& italic: Therefore they say unto God

As you can see, it is quite a stretch to really say these are companion fonts, but this disconnect has become the standard which we assume is correct by definition. The major thing to remember in all of this is that we are dealing with the popular leader and all of its copycat versions. There are hundreds of versions of Garamond. Garamond 3 (which we have chosen to use) is actually built off a type design by Jean Jannon in the seventeenth century. According to Alexander Lawson, Jannon's designs (which are directly derivative of Garamond's) are the principal source of most of what we see called Garamond. If you go back to the original, you can find wide room for variation.

None of this matters, as Garamond has become the standard by which all other serif font designs are judged, for most people. They all have certain characteristics as we have mentioned.

Garalde characteristics

- 🐭 An obvious Aldine base

- 🐭 Smaller x-height with corresponding increase in ascender and descenders

- 🐭 Hairline strokes are tapered with a flare toward the serifs at the end of the strokes

- 🐭 Wide concave serifs

- 🐭 An inconsistent axis: as in the a e & o. As you can see in the sample of Garamond 3 on the previous pages, the axis of the a is humanist, the o is nearly vertical and the e is sinister. This lack of rigid consistency is one of the reasons these fonts look so beautiful, human, and comfortable.

- 🐭 The counters of the a & e are very small: However, you can see that Garamond 3 didn't follow that convention.

Hoefler calls the overall look soft, though I have no idea to what he is referring specifically. Like all superstars, Garamond's virtues are vastly overrated. I guess I should just say it. I've never really liked Garalde letterforms. Many of the them look distorted to my eye. But I am certainly in the minority.

French Oldstyle: ITC Galliard

As mentioned, Granjon was another of the new breed of professional punchcutters who developed type foundries in Paris in the early sixteenth century. I find Matthew Carter's interpretation to be the best of the Garalde styles, but

Hoefler makes it another classification (probably just to give himself an excuse to show this exquisite design in addition to the required Garamond). It's much prettier.

French Oldstyle characteristics

- ❦ Heavier
- ❦ Serifs become much stronger: more like supports than finishing strokes to a stem
- ❦ Larger x-height
- ❦ Slightly closed aperture

Carter, who was involved in the cataloguing of Christopher Plantin's office in the 1950s, understands these differences very well. Plantin was basically the first type foundry conglomerate selling reproductions of various punchcutters' designs. Plantin was especially fond of Granjon's sense of style and included more than sixty of Granjon's designs. In fact, Plantin's collection has greatly added to our modern font knowledge.

Matthew calls Garamond's design "stately, calm, & dignified" in contrast to Granjon's "spirited, tense, & vigorous" stylings. It sounds like art historical balderdash to me, but maybe it helps you. This is some of the poopery I mentioned earlier that infests the type world.

ITC Galliard

ABCDEFGHI
JKLMNOPQ
RSTUVWXY
Z1234567890
abcdefghijklmn
opqrstuvwxyz

ITC Galliard is an adaptation of Matthew Carter's 1978 phototype design for Mergenthaler. Galliard was modeled on the work of Robert Granjon, a sixteenth-century letter cutter, whose typefaces are renowned for their beauty and legibility. *MyFonts*

Galliard certainly fit well (and had a causal effect) to the styles of the 1980s with the large x-heights and crisp, clean, rounded shapes. His shapes were a revelation to me personally and a major part of my style in the early eighties. Some people even see Granjon's influence in that modern megalith: Times Roman.

Dutch Old Style: Janson

By the 1600s, French oppression had caused the center of typography to shift from Paris to Antwerp primarily through Plantin who was based there. This style commercialized the French designs that were promoted by Plantin. The Dutch influence made the French work more printable, taking out some of the subtleties of Garamond and Granjon.

Dutch Oldstyle characteristics

Janson Text

ABCDEFGHI
JKLMNOPQ
RSTUVWXY
Z1234567890
abcdefghijklmn
opqrstuvwxyz

A faithful recreation of one of the great seventeenth century Dutch typefaces cut by the 'protestant Transylvanian Miklós Tótfalusi Kis. He was a Transylvanian protestant who, sent to Holland in the last quarter of the seventeenth century to learn printing, became one of the leading punchcutters of his time before returning to Transylvania to print bibles. His teacher, in Amsterdam around 1680, was Dirk Voskens. *MyFonts* Actually, we would call Kis Hungarian and his name is pronounced Kish—as the s is pronounced in Hungarian with the cs having the s sound.

- ❦ Serifs flattened & strengthened: with almost wedge-shaped brackets
- ❦ Modulation increased: there was quite a bit more stroke contrast
- ❦ Much thinner hairlines
- ❦ Darker, more compact
- ❦ Strong horizontal stress
- ❦ Ball terminals in the lowercase

Their main influence was in England where there really was no typefounding industry until Caslon in the eighteenth century. These styles were a complete abandonment of calligraphic roots. Mechanically constructed with new elements like the ball terminals of the a, c, g, r and so on. The bdpq characters are no longer based on the o. The diagonal strokes of the v, w, & y are sometimes bowed out to make for better letterspacing.

Lawson sums them up as "not as esthetically pleasing as the

French letters, but were more practical for the everyday production of commercial printing." The Stylistic Gestapo of the East Coast has downplayed these fonts as somehow lesser creations. Hoefler, on the other hand, says the Kis' forms had wonderfully smooth type color with "a typographic rhythm of such evenness" that it was unmatched in oldstyle fonts. The question is: Do you like it or not?

These fonts had huge influence on typography of the 17th and early 18th centuries. They were immensely popular, especially in England. Hoefler says that the English love of the fonts was two-fold: first they were attractive and sturdy—second they were necessary. The English Star Chamber (a secretive court) made newsbooks illegal. So they were all printed in Amsterdam and smuggled into England. Because of these and other restrictions to typefounding, there were no English typefounders throughout the 17th century.

English Old Style: Caslon

MyFonts puts it this way: "William Caslon released his first typefaces in 1722. Caslon's types were based on seventeenth-century Dutch old style designs, which were then used extensively in England. Because of their remarkable practicality, Caslon's designs met with instant success. Caslon's types became popular throughout Europe and the American colonies; printer Benjamin Franklin hardly used any other typeface. The first printings of the American Declaration of Independence and the Constitution were set in Caslon."

Adobe Caslon

ABCDEFGHI
JKLMNOPQ
RSTUVWXY
Z1234567890
abcdefghijklmn
opqrstuvwxyz

For her Caslon revival, designer Carol Twombly studied specimen pages printed by William Caslon between 1734 and 1770.

If Garamond isn't the standard, Caslon is.

English Oldstyle characteristics

❧ The end of calligraphic influence in oldstyle fonts

❧ No hint of cursive

❧ Letters built from interchangeable parts: they were assembled, much like you are going to do in Fontographer.

❧ Absolute verticals

Transitional: Baskerville

Baskerville

ABCDEFGHI
JKLMNOPQ
RSTUVWXY
Z1234567890
abcdefghijklmn
opqrstuvwxyz

John Baskerville had John Handy cut from his own brilliant designs, based on a lifetime of calligraphy and stonecutting. *MyFonts*

By the end of this period, fonts had appeared with a rigidly vertical axis (usually called a rational axis). You can see it in Baskerville above & left This was the time of the Revolution and design was into Retro classical, which was called Neoclassical by the historians. This is the time of Monticello. Franklin was extremely impressed with John Baskerville's designs in England at the time.

Transitional characteristics

❧ Rational axis: rigidly vertical

❧ Small bracketed serifs

❧ More modulation: to the place where the thins can break up if you're not careful

❧ Generous counters: look at the huge aperture on the lowercase

❧ Entirely horizontal stress

❧ Rational system of parts

Baskerville's influence on typography

Outside of John's very beautiful typeface, his major influence was on the general look of page layout and formatted typography. He liked Caslon's work but wanted to improve on it. He was an amateur printer and he made his press a hallmark of excellence. He used a brass plate and a hard impression when the fashion was a soft squeeze. He smoothed his papers by running them through heated copper cylinders, instituting what we now call calendaring. He used wide margins and well-leaded copy, beginning the quality style that we still use today.

Because he was an amateur, the pros copied his work relentlessly. Evidently you could steal anything not done by pros, maybe because they had no guild to protect them? He was largely unsuccessful in England but enthusiastically received by European craftsmen. As seen in fonts like New Baskerville, John's fonts are still a standard for typographic beauty. Though rational and mechanical, they are clear, easy to read, and elegant.

The entire oldstyle period

Through the 1500s, 1600s, and up to the mid-18th century, these oldstyle letter forms went through gradual changes. Punchcutters moved continuously away from the calligraphic roots of letter forms. As Europe was caught up in the extravagance and luxury of the Baroque and Rococo, those lavish curves and flourishes made their way into type design as well. But the influence was outside what we now consider the mainstream. It has only historical interest.

Type designs gradually became drawn rather than written. Baroque designers played with letter forms, having stems that varied in slope and bowls that varied in axis in the same font. The entire period was extravagant, but tightly based on classical old styles. The finishing portion of this entire period, which I am calling oldstyle, was populated with rigidly defined, carefully drawn forms. Throughout this period, careful adjustments were tried with axis, aperture, serif style,

"Oldstyle" Comparisions

Jenson
Hark! Toxic jungle water vipers quietly drop on zebras for meals.
AaBbCcDdEeGgHhK-kMmNnOoPpRrSsUu-WwYy1234567890

Caslon
Hark! Toxic jungle water vipers quietly drop on zebras for meals.
AaBbCcDdEeGgHh KkMmNnOoPpRrSs UuWwYy1234567890

Garamond
Hark! Toxic jungle water vipers quietly drop on zebras for meals.
AaBbCcDdEeGgHh KkMmNnOoPpRrSs UuWwYy1234567890

Galliard
Hark! Toxic jungle water vipers quietly drop on zebras for meals.
AaBbCcDdEeGgHh KkMmNnOoPpRrSs UWwYy1234567890

Bembo
Hark! Toxic jungle water vipers quietly drop on zebras for meals.
AaBbCcDdEeGgHh KkMmNnOoPpRrSs UuWwYy1234567890

Goudy Oldstyle
Hark! Toxic jungle water vipers quietly drop on zebras for meals.
AaBbCcDdEeGgHh KkMmNnOoPpRrSs UuWwYy1234567890

Minion
Hark! Toxic jungle water vipers quietly drop on zebras for meals.
AaBbCcDdEeGgHh-KkMmNnOoPpRrSs UuWwYy1234567890

Palatino
Hark! Toxic jungle water vipers quietly drop on zebras for meals.
AaBbCcDdEeGgHh KkMmNnOoPpRrSs UuWwYy1234567890

and so on. However, to our eye in the twenty-first century, all of these fonts are minor variations on a common theme.

Oldstyle fonts are still the normal choice for body copy. Your personal style will determine which you choose. The variations definitely have their own character and leave their feel in the documents that use them.

Beyond that, they are all old, traditional letterforms to us. The main point is that all of these fonts, to the contemporary eye, look very similar. More to the point, they all provoke nearly identical reader reactions (unless that reader is quite sophisticated graphically – with a trained eye). It is true there are major differences to the typographer's eye, but then there are not many of us. Functionally, these all can be used in the same places, for the same clients. The only differences are ones of taste & personal style.

Revolutionary styles (to locate them by time)

Modern: Bodoni Book

These are type styles of the late 1700s and early 1800s, although their influence remains. To call them Modern, as most of the schools do, is silly. They are 200 years old. To call them Romantic (as Bringhurst does) is equally strange for they are cold fish. They are the natural expression of the radical, revolutionary intellectualism of the period. They are built with hard, tightly structured letterforms which push out the emotional, warm, comfortable type of the Old Style fonts, replacing it with spiky, carved, structured forms. The Bodoni typestyles used fine hairlines which contrasted sharply with bolder stems, and the hairline serifs are often unbracketed (and very difficult to print).

Bodoni is often seen grouped together with the Frenchman Didot. But Didot's shapes were rigidly intellectual whereas, Bodoni favored Rococo ornament, slight bracketing of the serifs in the larger sizes and a much better sense of design. These fonts can be very beautiful, but never comfortable. Baskerville led into this but it is still a very conservative, oldstyle font when compared to these. Most touches of humanity are cleaned out of these styles. The best you can do is think of a severe elegance — a cold formality.

Modern (revolutionary) characteristics

- ❦ Serifs lose all bracketing: becoming thin, horizontal lines no thicker than the hairline strokes

- ❦ The aperture is shut down

- ❦ The axis is rigidly vertical

- ❦ Extreme stroke modulation

- ❦ Condensed

Bodoni Book

ABCDEFGHI
JKLMNOPQ
RSTUVWXY
Z1234567890
abcdefghijklmn
opqrstuvwxyz

Giambattista Bodoni of Parma, Italy, designed and cut his typefaces at the end of the eighteenth century. They are recognized by the high contrast, pure vertical stress, and hairline serifs. This particular version of Bodoni was first created by Morris Fuller Benton for American Type Founders. *MyFonts*

These fonts are associated with the Rococo period of art history, as mentioned. It is hard to reconcile (at least for me) the tightly controlled, rigidly refined shapes of Bodoni with the fashionable and extravagant stylistic excesses which define the Rococo. I see them as the complementary opposite—with the revolutionary styles controlled more by the intellectualism of the nineteenth century.

Fat Faces: Bodoni Poster

In the 19th century, a huge variety of decorative typefaces appeared for advertising use. Many of them we now simply call Display. Some we call circus fonts. They were also used for what we now call Western posters. Hoefler has two categories devoted to them, but they are really minor players. As a side note, Bodoni Poster really isn't radical enough to be called a Fat Face.

Slab Serif: Cheltenham

Several slab serif fonts were designed during the same time period that the Egyptian discoveries including King Tut were found. Egyptian things became the raging fashion in the world at the time. As a result, fonts from that period are often called Egyptians. As we'll see below, these became more prevalent as a style in the early 20th century.

MyFonts believes that Daniel Berkeley Updike provided the impetus for the architect Bertram G. Goodhue to design the prototype in 1896. He did that for Ingalls Kimball at the Cheltenham Press—hence the name. Morris Fuller Benton at ATF developed it into the increasingly popular design we know today over a half decade later.

Cheltenham

ABCDEFGHI
JKLMNOPQ
RSTUVWXY
Z1234567890
abcdefghijklmn
opqrstuvwxyz

"Owing to certain eccentricities of form," writes Updike, "it cannot be read comfortably for any length of time." But he concludes: "It is, however, an exceedingly handsome letter for ephemeral printing." *MyFonts*

Slab serif characteristics

- Even stroke weight with very little modulation
- The aperture is nearly closed
- Serifs: Largely unbracketed slabs with the same stroke thickness as the rest of the letterform
- Nothing stylish or ornamented: There are no small caps, oldstyle figures, ligatures, or any of the other graceful tools of traditional typography.

These fonts were designed in response to the overwhelming fashion of modern fonts that looked great at large sizes, but tend to fall apart in the smaller sizes needed for text. These are sturdy fonts that are surprisingly easy to read, even though they are clunky, and heavy. Mostly, unlike the Moderns, they printed well.

Geometric slabs: Rockwell

Rockwell

ABCDEFGHI
JKLMNOPQ
RSTUVWXY
Z1234567890
abcdefghijklmn
opqrstuvwxyz

"The original Rockwell was produced by the Inland type foundry in 1910, which issued it as Litho Antique; American Type Founders revived the face in the 1920s, with Morris Fuller Benton cutting several new weights."
MyFonts

This particular subset of slab serifs is more contemporary. Typical fonts of this type are Memphis, Rockwell, and City. The readability is usually very low. However, the serifs make these fonts a much better choice for readability than geometric sans fonts like Avant Garde, Century Gothic, Bauhaus, and even Futura.

These fonts are an outgrowth of the modernist movement of the early twentieth century. Here letter forms are constructed geometrically, most with purely circular bowls, no modulation, slab serifs, closed aperture, and so on. Intellectually, they could almost be considered the scientific extension of the socialist expression found in realism. Currently they are not common but many designers like them a lot. They are sort of manly, if you know what I mean.

Realist: Clarendon

Type for the common man—ignored by almost every classification system

This is a Bringhurst classification. In the mid-1800s, a type design movement began making type for the workers, the common man, the non-educated. Stylistically they are an extension of transitional forms. They were never really popular with designers, but they have had a lot of influence. Slab serif type, when the serif is bracketed, is sometimes referred to as a Clarendon. This font originated in England in 1845 and is named for the Clarendon Press in Oxford. It was intended to be a heavier complement to the more "ordinary" serif designs.

Many of these fonts were the result of readability studies of the time. As such they were used by newspapers. One of these fonts, Century Schoolbook, is the font many of us used when we learned to read in the first few grades of school. It may be the most elegant of the bunch. In general, heavy, clunky, and old-fashioned are the terms associated with fonts like these.

Clarendon
ABCDEFGHI
JKLMNOPQ
RSTUVWXY
Z1234567890
abcdefghijklmn
opqrstuvwxyz

Art Nouveau: Arnold Böcklin

Late 19th & early 20th Century

The swirling curves of Art Nouveau were also used to produce type. It seems like a rebellion against the realists, much like the entire movement was a rejection of contemporary morality and tradition.

These are the first fonts with little tie to traditional letterforms. They were never really popular, but certain cultures can take them on for a time. They were the absolute standard for the Spanish culture in New Mexico in the early 1980s, for example. An Art Nouveau font would be Arnold Böcklin, but Raphael is usually liked by the same people though it is not really from the same genre.

Fonts like these need to be used very carefully. From a design point of view, they are very interesting. However, they are usually quite hard to read. The larger problem, though, is their ties to a cultural movement known for its depravity. They are used a lot by writers and designers in the occult. You need to be aware of these issues.

Current synthesis: Veljovic

Many recent serif faces play with attributes of any and all historical styles. Often they experiment with distinctive serif stylings, sharp angular features, fanciful modulations. However, these more playful aspects are often very restrained and elegant. They take pieces from all over and show a wide variety from Times New Roman to Palatino to Veljovic. Often, like in Usherwood, the x-heights are very large – strictly a fashion statement from the 1980s.

Sans serif classifications

There are not nearly as many options in sans serif type. I am only going to give you four general types. I frankly invented these categories to help you make sense of what you run across in your search to build your own font library. Hoefler doesn't even cover them.

Current sans serif use is a really new phenomenon. The first really popular sans was Helvetica in the 1950s. It was a raging fashion and has become the most popular font in the world. That is very much like saying that the Ford F-150 pickup truck is the most popular truck in the world.

We are talking about functionality to a certain extent. But Helvetica is not really even functional. It is almost like comfort food and not much better for you typographically than Kraft Mac & Cheese is nutritionally.

Only very recently has there been a genuine move toward truly readable sans serif typefaces.

Gothic: Franklin Gothic

Sans serif typefaces started in the early 19th century with a single line mention of a monoline font in Caslon's last catalog. The original fonts were all caps. In Europe these are called grotesques. Around the turn of the 20th century, these fonts were very popular.

Franklin Gothic was designed by Morris Fuller Benton in 1902 as his version of the heavy sans serifs first made

popular by Vincent Figgins in 1830. They are the direct ances-
tors of Helvetica. They look a little old-fashioned, but to my
eye, at least, they look better.

Franklin Gothic
ABCDEFGHIJKLMNOPQRS
TUVWXYZ1234567890
abcdefghijklmnopqrstuvwxyz

Geometric Sans: Futura

These are largely a product of
radical modernism, the Bauhaus in
Germany, and the Art Deco movement of the 1920s and 1930s. The
letterforms seem to be absolute
geometric constructs, but they
often have many subtle adjustments beyond that to make them
more readable (but just barely).
After their introduction the use of
Gothics became unsophisticated—it
was just a fashion thing.

Futura
ABCDEFGHI
JKLMNOPQ
RSTUVWXYZ
1234567890
abcdefghijklmn
opqrstuvwxyz

Designed by Paul Renner in 1927,
Futura is the classic example
of a geometric sans serif type
based on the Bauhaus design
philosophy. *MyFonts*

The German Bauhaus tech-
nological school headed up by the
architect Walter Gropius was especially involved in pursuing revolu-
tionary new font designs. One of its instructors, Herbert
Bayer, developed a geometric sans with no normal C&lc
relationships. He advocated a character redesign to bring it
more into line with normal speech patterns—basic intellectual drivel with no contact to a normal reader's mind.

These fonts are very stylish and loved by a large portion of graphic designers. They are not really appropriate for
typographic use. The real problem with geometric fonts is
the readability issue. Because all of the bowls are perfectly

round and the aperture is usually almost closed, there is little visual difference between an a, c, e, or o. More than that, an ol looks a lot like a d, an rn can look identical to an m, and even a cl can seem to be a d. They can work fairly well in headlines, but using them for body copy is usually a serious mistake.

Locally, here in southern Minnesota, several of the local colleges have chosen to use Futura or its more radical cohort, Avant Garde, as the official font for their school. Their official documents may look "modern", but they certainly are difficult to read—which kind of misses the point, don't you think? Typical fonts are: Futura, Kabel, Avant Garde, Century Gothic, and Bauhaus.

Populist commoner: Helvetica
"Normal" fonts — the default
sans — neo-grotesques

Helvetica

ABCDEFGHI
JKLMNOPQ
RSTUVWXYZ
1234567890
abcdefghijklmn
opqrstuvwxyz

Helvetica was designed by Max Miedinger in 1957 for the Haas foundry of Switzerland (the name is derived from Helvetia, the Latin name for Switzerland). *MyFonts*

These are what I call the normal fonts—like Helvetica and Univers. (Arial/Geneva are the Microsoft/Apple versions of this classification.) Their "normality" comes from the simple fact that they are the default fonts in some word processors.

These are part of a large effort in the 1950s to clean up font families from the old Gothic styles and make them truly usable typographically. Most of them have many subtle curve adjustments, but the stroke is virtually unmodulated. The aperture is closed up tight in most of them, especially for the e.

In general, even the best of them "feel clunky", for lack of a better word. They are difficult to read—though very legible. They tend to cause what I call "bureaucratic" reactions in the reader—simply because so many bureaucracies require their use. Their ubiquitous, default usage has relegated them to the background noise of modern typographic style. There is no doubt, however, that Helvetica is the most popular font of the 20th century. Helvetica can be used well, but you have to be very careful.

These fonts were the raging fashion in the 1950s—especially Helvetica. For logo design, Helvetica Black almost took over the decade. They came to symbolize business—cool, objective, clean, and so on. There is even a movie named Helvetica (which is actually quite good). The font has recently been redesigned or modernized and called Helvetica Neue. Helvetica has become one of the most popular fonts of all time, running far up on MyFonts best seller list and on the list of Monotype's best sellers as well.

Stylized Sans: Gill Sans

The relatively friendly sans serif styles

This is what I am calling those fonts which have a style that seems relatively warm and friendly, even though there is little or no modulation of the stroke. Many type designers include these fonts in what is called the Humanist Sans classification, but they do not have the necessary characteristics. Without modulation there is no axis that could be called humanist.

Many of these fonts make relatively good body copy in short bursts. They all have a distinctively warm feel — relative to other sans serif faces. Common faces in this genre would be Gill Sans, Frutiger, Corinthian, Skia, and

Gill Sans

ABCDEFGHI
JKLMNOPQ
RSTUVWXYZ
1234567890
abcdefghijklmn
opqrstuvwxyz

Designed by Eric Gill and based on the typeface Edward Johnston designed in 1916 for the London Underground signage. *MyFonts*

Trebuchet – among many others. Myriad has become the Adobe default sans. They are very popular for good reason. Dell Computers used Gill Sans for quite a while to distance itself from the Helvetica of the typical business PC competitors, and to seem more friendly, warm and accessible.

Stylized Sans characteristics

- No modulation
- The character shapes have unique detail that gives these fonts a very personalized style
- Two-stage a and g are often used
- Only lining figures
- Very legible

Humanist Sans: Optima

Readable, modulated sans serif fonts for text

Optima

ABCDEFGHI
JKLMNOPQ
RSTUVWXYZ
1234567890
abcdefghijklmn
opqrstuvwxyz

Created in 1958 by Hermann Zapf for the Stempel foundry, Optima combines features of both serif and sans serif types into one humanistic design.
MyFonts

These fonts are actually neither fish nor fowl. Instead of serifs they tend to have slight flares, They have a modulated stroke and a humanist axis. They are the most elegant of the sans serifs. Most commonly available would be Optima, Poppl Laudatio, and Zapf Humanist.

Humanist sans serifs are radically growing in popularity. They are very readable. They have become the fashion for body copy in the new millennium. It remains to be seen if this is fashion or a radical change in our page layout formatting. Humanist sans serif typefaces are very clean, neat, and unobtrusive. They are increasingly chosen for use as body copy in contemporary design.

My personal best seller: Brinar

My most popular font, as far as sales is concerned, is a humanist sans. Brinar began as Deaconia—my take on Minister. The original serif font is owned by Linotype who writes that Minister was based on Garalde types with an oblique stress, wide caps, and strongly concave serifs. I have no idea which fonts he used for his inspiration.

I wrote this for MyFonts: "I've been working on a usable sans serif for body copy since the mid-1990s (though I certainly did not know it at the time)...Now it finally makes it to where I was headed all along as a sans text font. This is a well modulated humanist, sans serif font family with many OpenType features and over 600 characters: Caps, lowercase, small caps, ligatures, swashes, small cap figures, oldstyle figures, numerators, denominators, accented characters, ordinal numbers, and so on.

Brinar

ABCDEFGHI
JKLMNOPQ
RSTUVWXYZ
1234567890
abcdefghijklmn
opqrstuvwxyz

"It is designed for text use in body copy. But it also works very well for elegantly stylized display."

Current fashion

At present, sans serifs are very popular. It remains to be seen how long this lasts. It seems likely that sans serif usage will continue to grow. It wouldn't surprise me to find sans serifs more directly tied to certain niches of design, but there is really no way to tell.

The only things we know for sure: What we are doing today will look very dated by 2050. It will probably come back in style by the end of the century. That's how things go in fashion, as you know.

Sans Serif Comparisions

Franklin Gothic

Hark! Toxic jungle water vipers quietly drop on zebras for meals. AaBbCcDdEeGgHh KkMmNnOoPpRrSs UuWwYy1234567890

Helvetica

Hark! Toxic jungle water vipers quietly drop on zebras for meals. AaBbCcDdEeGgHh KkMmNnOoPpRrSs UuWwYy1234567890

Century Gothic

Hark! Toxic jungle water vipers quietly drop on zebras for meals. AaBbCcDdEeGgHh KkMmNnOoPpRrSs UuWwYy1234567890

Corinthian

Hark! Toxic jungle water vipers quietly drop on zebras for meals. AaBbCcDdEeGgHh KkMmNnOoPpRrSs UuWwYy1234567890

Frutiger

Hark! Toxic jungle water vipers quietly drop on zebras for meals. AaBbCcDdEeGgHh KkMmNnOoPpRrSs UuWwYy1234567890

Gill Sans

Hark! Toxic jungle water vipers quietly drop on zebras for meals. AaBbCcDdEeGgHh KkMmNnOoPpRrSs UuWwYy1234567890

Futura

Hark! Toxic jungle water vipers quietly drop on zebras for meals. AaBbCcDdEeGgHhKkMmNnOoPpRrSsUuWwYy1234567890

Brinar

Hark! Toxic jungle water vipers quietly drop on zebras for meals. AaBbCcDdEeGgHh KkMmNnOoPpRrSs UuWwYy1234567890

What about the rest of the type styles?

What about all the type that is outside the classifications we just covered? First of all, proportionally there isn't that much of it. Most of it is either serif or sans serif. However, there is huge variety—in every artistic style, for every historical period. Many are so rigidly categorized that they can hardly be used for anything else.

Decorative is probably the best term for this miscellaneous grab bag. Decorative type is defined as typefaces that are so highly styl-

Decorative

HERCULANUM

PRINCETOWN

Rubino Sans

ROSEWOOD

MESQUITE

Mona Lisa

ECCENTRIC

Abiquiu

ized that they cannot be read in body copy sizes. You need to be very careful in the use of these fonts. Legibility is the obvious problem.

That being said, this is where you usually look for fonts to be used for logo stylings. There are so many of these fonts in such a wide variety of styles that you can usually find a font that matches the personality of the company you are designing for. Of course, the font design is usually just the start as you modify the letters that make up the name into a logo worth remembering.

Mimicking handwriting

There are hundreds of fonts, maybe even thousands by now, that mimic hand writing. There are styles for every historical period and every cultural niche. They range from graffiti to impossibly elegant Spencerian scripts. The main thing to remember is that they are a new phenomena with virtually nothing in existence before the 20th century. In fact, they were so hard to produce for hot metal letterpress typography that they really didn't start appearing in large quantities until the advent of photographic production. Most of the new releases today are scripts.

Lawson makes a valiant effort at categorizing scripts, but it's really a waste of time. This is a category determined entirely by what you like:

- ❦ Calligraphic: flat-nibbed pen
- ❦ English Roundhand: Formal joining scripts
- ❦ Brush Scripts: Produced with a brush

We could add:

- ❦ Graffiti Scripts: spray can
- ❦ Marker Scripts: felt tipped pens
- ❦ Chalk Scripts: chalk and charcoal
- ❦ Pencil Scripts: and the list could go on & on

But these ignore attitude, style, period, history, & all the rest.

[DAKOTA]

Basically, you need to make sure you have what you need.

[CHALKDUSTER]

Does it fit your client's needs? [EDWARDIAN SCRIPT]

A good script can really add a strong sense of style to your work... [SPRING]

Starting to draw a new font

We are now finally ready to begin drawing the actual glyphs we are going to use for a brand new font design drawn from scratch. For me this changes every font. Some designers recommend that you start with specific letters like the H and maybe the O. You will see many suggestions over the years. Mine is simple:

Start with the glyph you have most formed in your head

There are many ways to start a glyph:

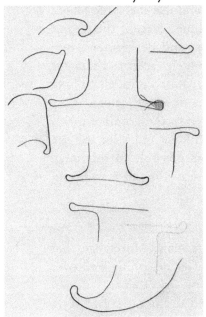

🐛 Sketch: A loose pencil or marker rough

🐛 Pieces: A sketchbook page of various pieces of the glyphs. You can see a scanned page from one of my sketchbooks to the left. But, I almost never use them— too crude & difficult to deal with. But I often use them as I develop a glyph that is causing my trouble.

🐛 Finished drawing: rendered characters in ink

🐛 A large sample: I often start with a printed sample of an old font, as we did with CushingTwo and Poniard.

🐛 Pen tool drawings: Duh! But then there are many people who draw in Illustrator. Cabarga's books are based on this technique— especially, the *Logo, Font, & Lettering Bible*.

❦ Glyphs from earlier fonts: Or false starts of a font design that make a new type of sense when you come back to them years later.

Scan & trace:

The first four examples above are begun with a scan into Photoshop. Here you need to work at high resolution. I usually use around 600 dpi greyscale. Once I get the Photoshop image cleaned up to black and white with minimal grays, I then place the scan into the outline window for that glyph. Fontographer will automatically paste the image into the Template layer where it will be shown as a dimmed image. It will automatically be scaled to the UPM size, unless you hold down the Shift+Option keys. Then it will be scaled to the baseline to ascender size.

The key to using scans well is to make sure you have the characters on the same baseline and use the same height of selection box. In Photoshop, marquee around the largest glyph leaving room for the ascender and descender. Then you can simply drag that marquee from character to character. Obviously, the glyphs need to be separated enough to take the marquee without showing pieces of other letters.

Once the scan is placed then go to the Element menu and choose Auto Trace. I'd start with Easy and 5 for the settings. Keep the tracings as simple as possible to minimize extraneous points. The better your scan (higher resolution) the tighter you can trace.

Don't limit yourself

As you can see, the options are many. More than that every font is different. In my case, after designing well over a hundred fonts, I can usually find pieces of already drawn fonts to start with. But you may well use a variety of techniques for various characters.

For me, the easiest way to convert a sketch is to open it in Photoshop, copy it, and paste it into a template layer of a blank outline window. I did that with the scan on the previous page. Then I carefully traced the shape I liked with the Pen tool. It depends on how comfortable you are with the Pen tool. I spent a half hour playing with this sketch. I am starting to get a feel for how it should look. But it's going nowhere right now. So, I started a new blank font I named IdeaStash. I'll keep the ideas there. After a decade, that idea has moved to the next level. The result you can see below. Who knows when it will actually be used in a font?

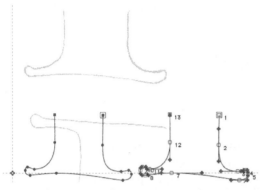

Dealing with scans & stuff

In my humble opinion, this is not generally a good idea. What you draw by hand is laborious to convert to paths. The conversion process seems to take the life out of the idea—for me.

The biggest problem with scanning and tracing is that it adds points where you do not expect them and creates far too many points, in general. You are adding a lot of path editing angst that I find less than inspiring. But that's me.

That being said, you all come from very different backgrounds and skill levels. You can read in Fontographer's manual, for example, how Judith Sutcliffe suggests you proceed in working calligraphically. I find her instructions incomprehensible because being left-handed makes calligraphy almost impossible [in my mind].

I suspect that many of you will draw in Illustrator, save as an EPS, and import that EPS into your outline window. That's fine, but again you need to be prepared to work harder than you must. The EPS I just imported (so I could talk about the process) converted all the nice curve points in AI to tangent points in FOG. You can also simply copy and paste from AI to FOG. Interestingly enough, the imported EPS went from baseline to ascender. The copy/pasted shape (the same one) went from descender to ascender. It did give me a path to play with, but that's not for me either. But then I really prefer to use a drawing tool designed for black and white shape creation—like Fontographer.

You simply need to learn to draw in Fontographer

Try many things. Plan to spend regular time—quite a bit of it. If you are still fighting the interface, you simply make extra work for yourself and at least some freedom of expression is missing from your designs. You need to go through the FOG manual and see if any of the options listed there excite you. Get comfortable with the software.

Developing a standard procedure

After spending so much time blathering about how you will all find your own way of working, I do have to say that there are some things that simply work. What I want to do is go through a general design procedure. We've covered all of it already, but I want to get it organized for you.

I will be drawing a lot on what Moye wrote in his Fontographer book. But of course I disagree with much of what he says. That's the nature of font design.

Make your major design decisions early

As we did with the fonts we produced so far, it starts with the Font Info dialog [Command+Option+F]. You can do nothing until you have made some decisions about the name of the font and its dimensions. The name you can redo at any point in the process (I do that all the time).

The dimensions, on the other hand, are a real pain to modify later. They are what controls the entire look of the font. You will do well to stick with a thousand unit em square. You need some decisions about ascender, cap height, x-height, and descender. Moye suggests leaving an extra 100 to 200 emus above the ascender to hold diacritical marks. There is no right or wrong, but I talked about the options quite a bit as we started CushingTwo.

If you have some drawn characters, make careful measurements. Remember what I did with the scan of Cushing No. 2 as we began CushingTwo. The key is to accurately convert the feel and style of your inspiration into an x-height, stem weight, axis, and modulation combination upon which you can build.

Don't be too precious

You must keep the design fluid as you begin. I don't think I have ever realized my early vision. As soon as I start the actual drawings, things change. This is part of the process. If you get too hung up trying to precisely realize what you think you see in your head, on the scan, in the drawing, or whatever, you'll squeeze the life out of your design.

I find this to be one of the few absolutes I can share. *Start drawing!* As you go through the process of drawing the basic characters upon which you will build the font the design will fall into a rhythm, develop a style, become a unique expression of your creativity.

Drawing tips

- ☙ Use orthogonal handles: I use this 50¢ word to simply get your attention. Orthogonal handles are vertical and horizontal. In most cases they are extrema. You will find that it often pays to hold down the Shift key as you manipulate or create handles. Fonts are dependent upon orthogonal handles to hint the width of the stems, for example. Hinted TrueType fonts will be around for a while yet—until the PC world upgrades their monitor quality and drawing routines on the screen.

🐭 Eliminate everything but the extrema: this is a
subset of the first point. As I mentioned several
times already, it is often the best procedure to
merge a point on a curve and then use Clean
Up Paths to add the appropriate extrema.

🐭 Keep your paths as simple as possible: I have found
over the years that I can almost always merge
any points between the extrema. Merging a
point seems to "capture" the curve with the
handle lengths of the extrema. If I need a point
between I add it, but carefully and regretfully.

🐭 Look for pieces you can share with
other glyphs: Consistency is a really
important virtue of the process.

An order of creation

I want to review the order in which you begin a font.
We've covered my practices, but intellectually there are reasons to do it differently than what I have shared so far. It
makes sense to draw the characters in a certain order.

The cap I

This is where you set the weight and the size and
shapes of the serifs or stem ends. The interplay between
stem and serif is one of the key determining factors in the
look of a font. Cut off the serif pieces and add them to your
pieces glyph. Draw a weight ball for the stem weight and
store it also.

The cap V

This is Moye's suggestion, and I think it is a good
one. I've never done it in this order and I've always felt I
was flailing about when it came to the serifs on the slanted
arms of the A, K, V, and so on. Moye suggests using this to
set your minimum and maximum weights. In my experience
that might work, but I doubt it. They would only work if the
angles line up with the axis—which would mean that they

would need to be at right angles with each other. I will be using it to design my serif shapes, and a general feel about the weights. By the way, it is a rigid norm that the left arm is wide and the right arm is narrow, in case you were wondering. I will also be adding these arm pieces to the pieces glyph.

The cap O

This is where you decide about the axis and modulation. Even if you are trying to emulate the variance in axis found in some of the baroque fonts, the weights are based on the O. Draw your minimum and maximum weight balls and store them in the pieces slot.

The cap P

As I was reviewing Moye's book this one surprised me, but it makes sense. You start with the cap I and expand the bowl out from that. This is the first place you start to decide about the crossbar height which is the third major determining factor of the font's style after the serif/weight decision and the axis/modulation decision.

This is also where you decide about closing the bowl. In many fonts the P is not closed and how you handle that terminal will shape the terminals and arm-ending serifs throughout your font.

The bowl of the P is usually larger, or at least taller, than the bowls of the B or R. Its weights are determined by the weight balls, of course. However, there is that special situation where the top of the bowl blends into the top serif. The weight there will be a little larger than the minimum, but it is usually smaller than the stem weight.

 Stop here & examine where you are: Moye makes this a special point and I agree with his emphasis. He says it this way, "Do not go beyond this point until you are satisfied with every aspect of these first four letters." However, you have to keep the font design fluid in order for it to fit your vision. It is an important assessment time, though—use it wisely.

Now go through the same procedure with the same letters in lowercase

For the same reasons, you need to make the lvop characters. The only addition is the special time you need to spend with the lowercase h. The shoulder on the h is another key determining factor in the font's style. The graceful blending of the arc of the shoulder into the side of the stem is crucial to your understanding of what you began with your serif design. It's quite possible what you decide here will be redirected into changes with the bracketing of your serifs and therefore to the shapes of your terminals.

Letter construction tips

After you have the nine basic letters drawn, the construction of the rest of the letters is relatively simple. All your decisions are basically made. Now you need to focus on consistency of vision.

- ❦ The cap H: Two cap Is and a crossbar. Sometimes the right stem is flipped horizontally (if you have asymmetrical serifs). The crossbar is another key determining factor of style. It normally determines the height of the middle strokes of letters like the B and E. Plus, it gives you the location of the arm intersection with the stem for the K. The width of the H is commonly about 75% of the cap O. The crossbar is almost always higher than the vertical center of the glyph.

Crossbar width: This is another stroke width you need to determine. In most cases a crossbar will be a little more than the minimum, but definitely less than the stem weight. You may well need a fourth weight ball.

- ❦ The cap W: Use two Vs to build this. You've seen that I normally lower my center serif. That is very unusual. There is wide room for variance here. Examine Ws in comparable fonts and set it up to match the feel of your vision for the font.

❦ The cap D: Moye says to use the I and the right half of the O. In my experience this is far too narrow in most cases. One of the determining factors in a D is the vertical location of the right extrema of the bowl. It can be higher or lower than the vertical center. I usually tie that height into the location of my crossbar on the H.

❦ The cap K: take the slanted arms from the V, which you have stored in your pieces component. The arm intersection varies a lot and it is commonly quite high. The character has about the same width as the H so the arms will be more vertical in most cases. Usually, the arms are nearly at a right angle to each other.

❦ The cap U: Moye says two Is and add the curve. I cut off the bottom serifs, use the bottom of the O narrowed to fit, and then resize the right stem to the minimum. It's almost always a little more narrow than the left stem even for monoline fonts.

❦ The Cap L, E, & F: Start with the stem and draw the arm of the L. The weight is the crossbar weight. The length is a little less than the width of the H. The terminal serif is yet another style determiner. I save the arm in my pieces component. The upper arm of the E&F is a flipped version of the lower arm, slightly shorter, and the terminal serif is usually a little more vertical. The middle crossbar of the E is the shortest of the three with a stylish serif. This crossbar is often shortened a bit for the F.

❦ The cap T: The cross beam is two copies of the top arm of the E with the cap I for the stem. The width of the character is about the same as the H.

❦ The cap B: Build it off the cap P flipped vertically, adjusting the crossbar to match the H. The top bowl is also a little more narrow. Take a bowl from another P and adjust it to fit. It takes careful weight adjustments.

- ❦ The cap C & G: This is built off the cap O with the top arm terminal of the E. The G commonly uses the top cap serif for its terminal. But it is almost always asymmetrical.

- ❦ The cap A: Rotate the cap V and add a crossbar—often a little lower than the normal crossbar height to help keep the counter open. If there is a top serif, it is built off the normal top of the cap stem. But there is room for a lot of style variation

- ❦ The cap M: Moye says to use two rotated Vs and then make the outside stems more vertical. The problem is the top serifs of an M are not found on the bottom of a V. Plus, they usually have heavily modified interior portions. In fact, the interior portions of the top serifs are commonly deleted and the outside stems are often vertical.

- ❦ The cap N: Moye says to build it off the V. I use two Is set to the width of the H. I narrow them to the minimum weight. I then delete the interior serif top left and the entire serif bottom right. The diagonal is drawn at the maximum weight. The bottom right point goes to the overshoot.

- ❦ The cap R: Add a tail to the P. BUT! I usually raise the crossbar to the normal crossbar height, and make the tail with only an outside serif using the thin arm of the V (if I use any serif at all). The tail sticks out beyond the bowl on top.

- ❦ The cap X: Use the arm pieces of the V. Place once and move the serifs together a little. Place again and rotate for the bottom serifs. Connect the serifs top left to bottom right at the thicker V weight and top right to bottom left at thinner weight. The top serifs are moved closer together to make the intersection higher than the centerpoint. I often have to cut out the center and hand draw the crossing stems attaching the two serif pairs. Remove Overlap to finish the character.

- ❦ The cap Y: The cap I with the top cut
  off merged with the two arms of the V.
  Move the arms toward the center until
  the overlap is near the centerpoint. Close
  the shapes and remove the overlap.

- ❦ The cap Z: The lower arm you have saved plus
  the flipped upper arm from the E connected by
  a maximum (or the thick V arm) weight stroke.
  The character is about the width of the H.

- ❦ The cap S: Difficult to build. The upper
  curve is smaller than the lower curve.
  The diagonal is close to the maximum
  weight—depending on the axis.

The lowercase letters

To review, we now have a component filled with pieces:
the two top serifs (cap and ascender), one or two bottom
serifs (caps and lowercase), the two top serifs of the V and
the bottom arm of the E—plus the three to five weight balls.
We have also designed the lhvop characters. We got the top
lowercase serif from the l and used the l to start the h.

- ❦ The lowercase n: Take the h and drop the top serif.
  It will take some reshaping. I commonly cut the
  top left corner of the outside edge of the p and
  save the this new top serif into the component.

- ❦ The lowercase m: combine two n s. The middle
  serif is often minimized or eliminated.

- ❦ The lowercase r: Start with an n. Cut off the right
  stem and the right third of the shoulder. Shape
  the new terminal. You may want to use this
  terminal for the c, the a, and maybe the s. I've
  been known to use something similar for the top
  arm of the k. These lowercase letters will usually
  not take a full arm terminal like the caps will.

- ❦ The lowercase d: a rotated p with the new top
  serif. The top serif is commonly unique to
  this glyph. The bottom serif is built off the

bottom stem serif with the bottom flattened and left side moved to the right a bit.

❦ The lowercase b: Start with an l and the o. If the bottom of the bowl of the p is open, then the bottom of the b may need to be opened also—using the same terminal.

❦ The lowercase q: A rotated b with a new top serif and only the right side of the bottom serif (commonly moved, angled, or slanted up a bit). The top serif may be modified toward the style of the ear on the g.

❦ The lowercase c: This is built off the o with the right side cut off and the terminal from the r or a reduced terminal from the cap C added on top. The bottom is a tapered point, often with a trimmed tip, sometimes with a minimal serif or beak.

❦ The lowercase e: This is built off the c. The crossbar is a little higher than the center and the tail is a little shorter than the width of the crossbar in most cases.

❦ The lowercase u: Often this is simply a rotated n. However, the bottom of the serif commonly needs to be flattened onto the baseline.

❦ The lowercase a & g: These are usually some of most unique portions of the font. There really are no rules for either the two-story or single story versions. I commonly build single-story a s from a d and single story g s from a rotated b, but the variances are too large. This is a place for personality within the constraints of your vision.

The lowercase g has some semi-rules. The upper bowl is above the baseline and smaller than the lower bowl. If the upper bowl is circular the lower bowl is usually oval. The oval bowl is always wider than the upper bowl.

❦ The lowercase t: The crossbar is at the x-height. The top never has a serif, but there is wide latitude for style. The tail of the t is often unique to the font—not used anywhere else.

❦ The lowercase v, w, & y: These are built directly off the cap V with slightly narrower serifs. The tail of the y is another place for personality.

❦ The lowercase x: This is built the same way as the cap X but using the serifs of the lowercase v.

❦ The lowercase i & j: This is the l shortened with the period centered above. The bottom half of the j is another place for limited personality. It may have a terminal based on the r terminal in your component.

❦ The lowercase z: Slide the upper arm of the cap Z down the diagonal, then shorten both arms to make the character the width of the n. The upper arm is shorter.

❦ The lowercase s: Have fun! This has the same problems as the cap S with the addition that three horizontals need to fit within the x-height. The upper bowl is a bit smaller—sometimes quite a bit.

Number construction tips

❦ The zero: This is usually more narrow than the cap O, unless the cap O is narrow. Then the zero is commonly nearly circular. There should be a clear difference between the two. The zero normally sets the width of all the numbers except the one. Oldstyle figures have more varied widths.

❦ The one: The upper arm is an arm, not a modified serif. You may need a small bulge on the right side of the top to bear the weight of the arm.

❦ The two: This should use the terminal from the r and the arm from the E. The upper bowl has the curves from the bowl of the P.

❦ The three: This uses the serifs from the S, but the terminal from the r can work better on top. The top bowl is always smaller—vertically at least.

❦ The four: The bottom serif on the bottom and the serif from the middle stroke of the e on the end of the crossbar.

❦ The five: Unique, but the bowl is the x-height.

❦ The six: The bowl is usually the x-height and the terminal is from the cap C.

❦ The seven: The arm from the cap Z. The diagonal stem is often curved and sometimes curved to vertical with an almost normal bottom serif. Normally there is no serif on the bottom.

❦ The eight: The upper bowl is smaller, diagonal from upper left to lower right is maximum, and the diagonal from the lower left to upper right is minimum. The key is getting the diagonals to cross each other as a single continuing line as in the X.

❦ The nine: A rotated six, but it usually needs a weight check. The bowl is commonly a little smaller than the bowl of the six to prevent top heaviness.

We did the oldstyle figures earlier and the small cap numbers. The punctuation and special characters have been discussed a little, but they are simply required to look *normal* in the context of type set using the font. Sorry, but you are the arbiter of normal for your font.

One of the best sources is wikipedia

Just Google the letter or character name and choose the wikipedia entry. You'll find a wealth of information and links. That's it.

Now you're a font designer. Have fun!

Appendix A:
Advanced Letterspacing

You will find many fonts require more than can be provided by the Auto Space capabilities. If you are going to sell your fonts, you will feel compelled to be much more careful with your spacing. But there are some things you need to know first, so you can decide how to work.

I do not want you to think that Fontographer cannot do good hand spacing of a font. It can. The Metrics window is clean, high resolution, and easy to understand. But, the process does take time.

However, there is a middle road that you might want to try. This involves hand spacing the caps and lower case, then building the components. Then auto spacing everything else. And finally you auto kern the entire font. Regardless, you need to learn to hand space.

Professional letterspacing

If you want to do all your hand spacing in Fontographer have no fears. The software has excellent tools for the job. I will show you how to do this here.

Web fonts: On the other hand, as long as I have to break up my OpenType fonts into two and a half 8-bit TrueType fonts for use by the web fonts distributors, I will auto space those versions of the fonts, and auto hint as well. Kerning is not used on the Web yet, so there is no need to bulk up the file sizes with kerning data. I do an Oldstyle version with oldstyle figures. A SmCaps version with small caps for the lowercase. Plus, a SmCapFigures version with small caps and the small cap figures.

I sell these all as a package for each font weight. This arrangement will surely change as the rest of the popular browsers catch up to the lead presently held by FireFox, in the use of OpenType fonts and kerning.

Hand letterspacing fonts

Basic methodology

Moye got this from a man named Walter Tracy. I'll show you how to add letterspacing by hand as you draw the characters. First, let's go through his process so you can use it as you hand space.

First we distinguish between 3 types of glyphs

1. Those with perfectly vertical sides
2. Those with sloping sides
3. Those with curved sides

The basic idea is that sloping or curved sides intro-duce additional white space and as a result need to be drawn closer to the edge—that is, that sidebearing needs to be reduced a skosh. The S and s do not really fit these 3 classes because of the internal spacing and terminal shapes involved—but they are often closer to #2. The rest work pretty well.

Remember, all this happens before kerning: At this point we are talking about *normal* letterspacing for either text or display. Kerning happens after this is taken care of. In fact, kerning is done after all the glyphs are completed for the entire font.

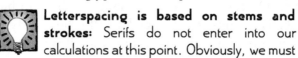 **Letterspacing is based on stems and strokes:** Serifs do not enter into our calculations at this point. Obviously, we must leave enough room so that the serifs do not bump unto each other or the glyph next to it. However, serifs are incidental to the spacing of the font—they only confirm that you have done a good job.

Moye says that most people (and I had not been one until I wrote the original *Practical Font Design* in FontLab) start their letterspacing with the O and the H—because they have the smallest and largest sidebearings, respectively. I don't use this any more, but it will introduce us to the Metrics panel.

Fontographer's Metrics panel

This is a clean and simple panel. For now, let's start with the Os & Hs. The manual says to start with equal spacing on both sides of your letters. Mine are set at 35 emus.

Letterspacing: Hs & Os

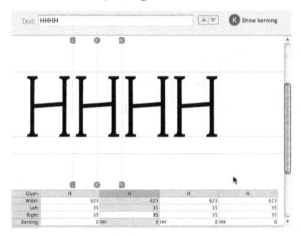

First, start by opening a New Metrics Window under the Window menu or type Command+K

Type four Hs into the Text field:

Here Stephen says to carefully adjust the spacing until you are happy, but it looks OK to me now with the 35 emus on both sides. This gives you the basic sidebearings for characters with vertical stems.

Clear the entry field and type in HOHOH:

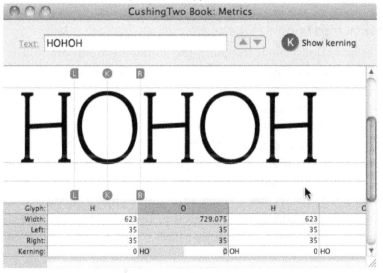

We're told by Moye to adjust the spacing around the O carefully. But this doesn't look too bad either. Because of the repeating pattern it usually does look fine.

So, next we try HHOOHH

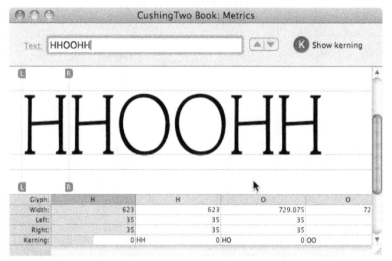

Now it looks pretty poor. I'm not sure what to do. If the HH and OO are OK, then the HO and OH are too wide. The OO looks the tightest. I need help. Basically what you are looking for is a pair of measurements for the vertical stems and the round sides.

Let's look at traditional setups

Stephen/Tracy suggests using the following numbers and setups (with the figures I would use for CushingTwo in the right column).

1 =	Sidebearing of H	90
2 =	A little less than H	60
3 =	Half sidebearing of H	45
4 =	Sidebearing of O	30
5 =	Minimum sidebearing	15

3 and 4 will always need some adjusting to make them work. This is fairly tight spacing, not quite text spacing, but looser than display spacing. For a text face, I use something closer to this:

1 = Sidebearing of H   120
2 = A little less than H   100
3 = Half sidebearing of H   60
4 = Sidebearing of O   45
5 = Minimum sidebearing   15

Then a good approximation of letterspacing is achieved using these figures as follows:

₅A₅   ₁B₄   ₄C₃   ₁D₄   ₁E₃

₁F₅   ₄G₂   ₁I₁   ₅J₁   ₁K₅

₁L₅   ₂M₁   ₂N₂   ₁P₄   ₄Q₄

₁R₅   ₄S₄   ₅T₅   ₁U₂   ₅V₅

₅W₅   ₅X₅   ₅Y₅   ₃Z₃

This is assuming a normally wide serif of 70-90 emus. It just takes practice. There is no right or wrong. But we need to talk about this in a bit.

So, let's plug in those figures

The easiest way is to use the Metrics panel itself. To can see the setup below. A-Z is typed into the entry field.

You click in either the left or right sidebearing field for the cap A. Then use tab to go to the next character and the Up or Down arrows to switch between Left and Right. I set them all in as listed and you can see the result above.

The bad pairs at a glance are AB, BC, RS, ST, and these are just the immediately obvious ones. Let me give you some of my "normal" adjustments. Many of these letters always have the same issues. So, you can usually simply adjust before kerning.

Typical adjustments to spacing

- The A is always a problem because of the slope: I set this very tight at right. You need to cut some of the spacing built into the following character.

- The F & G always have a gap: but this is a kerning pair so it's not set now.

- The tail of the J is a descender and it hooks to the left beyond the top serif: Remember, the left sidebearing is measured from the furthest left extrema. I set that at 20 on the left to keep the stems right. Actually, I set this up with the guides I will talk about in a bit.

- The L commonly needs to zero out on the right.

- The M is like the H: but not for slanted stems. In this case, I ended up with 60 left and 60 right.

- The P commonly needs to zero out on the right.

- The UV is a kerning pair, done later.

- The X commonly needs to zero out on one or both sides.

The second adjustment is much better. With that out of the way, we need to turn to the lowercase. The process is the same. The lowercase sidebearings are adjusted in exactly the same way.

2a1	1b4	4c3	4d1	4e4
1f3	4g2	1i1	3j1	1k4
1l1	1m1	1n1	1p4	4q1
1r5	3s3	1t2	1u1	5v5
5w5	5x5	5y5	3z3	

- Round shoulders need less space (h m n): about 15 less

This varies a lot by font

As I was getting the second edition of the FontLab book ready for release, I was working on Cutlass and the lettershapes were a bit unusual. Let's take a quick look.

Some things are obvious. For example, the AV&W are spaced more like a normal O. The Y is closer to the spacing of the S. But it goes much further than that. We can really see some of the more major differences when we look at the H and I. Here we see a first issue is the asymmetrical top serif. Plus, the H has an extended cross bar—on both sides. These little things really mess up spacing.

Below you can see that we obviously have many more issues here because of the unique letter shapes: I was surprised at how much the little crossbar extension messed up spacing with the O. There were many other adjustments to be made.

The bottom line is that you need to carefully analyze the fit of all your letters. There never is a standard solution.

For Cutlass the figures I started with were:

1 =	Right sidebearing of I	55
2 =	Right sidebearing of H	50
3 =	Left sidebearing of I	40
4 =	Sidebearing of O	30
5 =	Minimum sidebearing	20
6=	Zero or negative sidebearing	

Cutlass is a display font so it needs to be much tighter than what we are using for CushingTwo. But that's the whole point. Every font has a letterspacing that looks right for it. Only you know what looks right for a given font that you design. It is part of the design itself. Be careful about taking too much outside advice. They do not have the internal vision for the font that you do.

4A4   3B4   3C6   3D4   3E6

3F6   3G1   3H2   3I1   3K6

3L6   3M1   3N2   4O4   3P4

4Q6   3R6   4S4   5T5   1U4

3V3   3W3   5X5   1Y4   3Z1

As mentioned, the real controlling factor here is that fact that Cutlass is obviously a display font that will only be used at larger point sizes. That fact means that the letterspacing must be quite a bit tighter than it does for text type in the 9–12 point range.

abcdefghijklmnopqrstuvwxyz

As you can see there were some special issues with the lowercase also. But that is what makes font design interesting and challenging. In fact, while looking at the capture above I saw I needed to go back and fix quite a few things in the lowercase. It took quite a bit of adjustment. You also need to decide whether it is the letterspacing or the kerning that is causing the problem. It really needs hand kerning.

As I mentioned, it is really important to do this with the 62 character alphabet before you assemble the composites and carefully adjust the letterspacing until you are satisfied. You can type in the combinations that bother you in the text field. Type in sample words and randomized letter combinations. Take enough time to get it right.

Display or Text?

As I briefly mentioned above, letterspacing changes with the point size. In fact, if you have read any of my books on formatting, you realize that leading varies a lot with point size also. What is necessary spacing for ten point body copy looks absolutely humongous at seventy-two point.

It naturally follows that text faces—those designed to be used for formatting body copy—need quite a bit more letterspacing than display fonts that will be used only for larger headlines and subheads.

For *Practical Font Design: Part Two*, I went much more traditional

That book is about the design of an 8-font text family for book design which I named Contenu (it's the font family used to set this book). It is where I learned much of what I shared for CushingTwo. The weights ranged from Contenu Book to Contenu Black and they were all set much wider. I researched common text fonts and found the sidebearings were closer to what you see below. The sidebearings ignore the serifs and space from the vertical stems.

1 = Sidebearing of H   120
2 = A little less than H   100
3 = Half of H   60
4 = Sidebearing of O   45
5 = Minimum sidebearing   15–30

For many of the characters, these figures cannot be added in the Metrics window

There is a major conceptual problem with the Metrics window itself. The Metrics window measures from the left edge of the letter shape to the right edge. So, the serifs are included in the shape width. As I hope you recall, I quoted Moye (at the beginning of the first chapter on letterspacing in this book) saying, "Principal shapes (like stems) are used to judge letterspacing. Serifs, when present, are used to *confirm* good letterspacing." In reality, we need to ignore the serifs as we space and set the sidebearing numbers from the stems.

This problem is exacerbated by characters like J & j in which the hooking tail at the bottom of the character has no affect on letterspacing if it lies below the baseline. A two-story g has spacing problems if you base the spacing on the larger oval below the baseline—and that is what the Metrics window does. We've already talked about the problems with unusual character shapes. This means we need to letterspace as we go—while designing the characters.

Letterspacing as you draw

I have found that the only real solution is to set the sidebearings of each letter, number and symbol as I draw them. Once you begin doing this on a regular basis, the figures I gave you in the grids earlier in this chapter are memorized and become part of your understanding of character design.

I use two techniques to accomplish this: a set of guides one the left to set the left sidebearings and a measurement tool added to the pieces component.

Setting up sidebearing guides for the left side

What I do is simply add guides, measured from the baseline origin point, for each of the figures chosen for the spacing grid we just talked about. So, I add vertical guides at 15, 30, 45, 60, 90, & 120 emus to my templates. I vary these locations according to what I decide for the particular font. I tend to design font families for text use, so these are a good start. If I am doing a display font, these guide locations are heavily modified, as we saw with Cutlass.

With those guides in place it is a simple matter to select the entire character when it is completed and move it sideways to set the left sidebearing according to the numbers in the letterspacing grid we have been discussing. Obviously, because all characters have different widths, this does not work for the right sidebearings.

Adding a measurement tool for the right side

My solution, as usual, is to add a tool in the component slot. You can see what I use on the next page. I usually put it right next to the weight balls—between them and the origin line. By doing this, the tool is there for every letter I design. This works really well for the right sidebearing. It's nothing special, but it works. I left a copy of it in the ll slot of the fog template we used to start CushingTwo. If you use it, I think you'll find it works. I normally measure the right sidebearing from the extrema furthest to the right within the x-height. I say that because swashes commonly extend beyond the sidebearings. These swash extensions usually extend below the baseline.

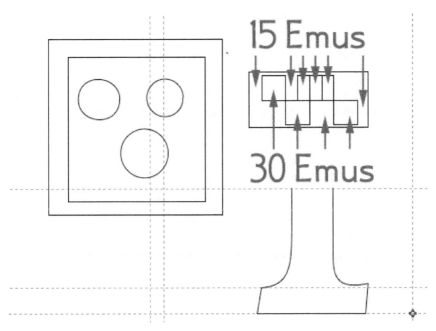

Both the left and right sidebearings take some practice, but after a couple of fonts, you start recognizing the issues as you design and make appropriate adjustments. You quickly find that for letters like the J or the j the left sidebearing must be measured from the left edge of the stem. For a two-story g, the sidebearing is determined by the upper bowl using the same settings the same as the o. For more unusual decorative letter shapes, you'll just develop a sense of what is required.

The elephants in the room

I recognize that all of your options will be constrained by the time you have available. Your decisions will also be affected by what usage you have planned for the font. Fin ally, you need to consider that you may need to use different options for Web fonts as opposed to high resolution print fonts. You have several options:

1. Auto space and auto kern everything: In this scenario, you do not need to worry about the hand spacing with guides mentioned above. The automatic processes will completely change any spacing adjustments you set up any way.

2. Auto space or hand space with no kerning: Turn on auto hinting for the export of TrueType fonts for use on the Web.

3. Hand space the basic alphabet and auto space the rest. Then auto kern the entire font: Here you can use the guides to set up the A–Z, a–z, and the figures (if you want them proportionally spaced). Read the "what you need to remember" section which follows this list.

4. Hand space everything as you draw. Carefully finish the letterspacing and kerning in Fontographer: Using the guides will eliminate most of hand adjustments in the Metrics window except for the kerning.

Kerning text file: I have a text file which I use in FontLab that has all my kerning pairs and spacing problems. It is nine pages and has 304 lines. You'll need to hand type (or copy/paste) every line into the Metrics palette. But, it will at least give you a good idea of the letter combinations you'll need to worry about. I'll put a link to it on the book page at the Hackberry site.

What you need to remember

For the third choice: Auto Space completely scrambles the hand spacing made with the guides. As far as I can tell, Fontographer sets a standard minimal left sidebearing and adjusts the right sidebearing to do its auto spacing. But I have never been able to figure it out. As a result, I would only hand space the caps, lowercase and numbers. Then after the font is drawn, select all glyphs you did not hand space and auto space them. Auto kerning will not mess this up.

Using the Metric Panel

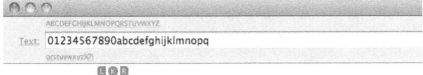

Glyph:	0	1	2	3
Width:	554.062	269	491	463.498
Left:	46	45	45	30
Right:	45.062	45	45	45
Kerning:	0 01	0 12	0 23	0 3

There are a couple of features here you need to understand. One of the really important ones is the ability to use a text file for your spacing. As you can see above, this enables you to add text strings that you can click through to adjust your spacing. If you look above the field which shows the current line (01234567890abcdefghijklmnopq), you can see a link for the previous line (ABCDEFGHIJKLM-NOPQRSTUVWXYZ). Below the field is a link for the next line (qrstuvwxyz%?!). These are the 2nd through 4th lines of my text file I use for kerning (the one I gave you a link for off my Fontographer page on the Hackberry Fonts Website.

 Keep it where you can find it: Every time you launch Fontographer each day, the text file will be gone. So, you need to keep it where you can find it easily.

If you look in the spreadsheet below the letter preview, check out the numbers below the one. You can see that the character in 269 emus wide, with a left sidebearing of 45 and a right sidebearing of 45, with zero kerning between the zero and the one.

You need to spend some serious time letterspacing these three lines

Do not set any kerning yet! We must get the letterspacing correct. First we need to adjust our numbers. The figures we used are not doing us any good here. It is common for me to set everything up and then start looking in the Metric panel only to discover that the figures I chose are not working. This is no big deal, but we must fix them. If you recall, the figures we used we these:

1 =	Sidebearing of H	120	(actual 75)
2 =	A little less than H	100	
3 =	Half sidebearing of H	60	
4 =	Sidebearing of O	45	(actual 55)
5 =	Minimum sidebearing	15	

What is throwing me off is the first number, the side-bearing of the H. I need to measure carefully in the outline window of the H and find out what the actual measurement is between the furthest left point and the origin. I select the point and look up on the measurement bar at the top of the outline window and I see that this point is actually 75 emus from the origin. I have noted that above.

So, what I want to do is actually type in the true numbers, with the changes. I double-click on the left sidebearing number for the A. I type in 15. Then I hit the down arrow to go to right sidebearing and type in 15 again. Then I type Tab to take me to the B. I type in 55 for the right, use the up arrow to select the left and type in 75. Tab to the C. 55 for the left and 60 for the right. I go through all 25 letters like this and type in the numbers. Here's the original with the first set of new numbers below.

ABCDEFGHIJKLMNOPQRSTUVWXYZ
ABCDEFGHIJKLMNOPQRSTUVWXYZ

Hopefully, you can see (I know it's hard) that the basic spacing is improved quite a bit. There is still too much space to the right of the G. The minimum space of 15 [ALRVWXY] seems too tight. I want to change the minimum to 30.

KLMNOPQRSTUVWX
KLMNOPQRSTUVWX
KLMNOPQRSTUVWX

The second adjustment looks quite a bit better at size. I'm sorry the captures look so bad. Remember, I'm looking at it 15 inches wide on my screen. Now I need to do the same thing for the numbers, lowercase letters, symbols, and small caps. We are looking to make the spacing look smooth and even.

 What you are looking for: The first few lines of type in the kerning text file are simple alphabets where you can see the letters in situations where kerning is not needed.

Especially for text type, this is a learned skill. The letters on the screen are huge. You have no control, but make the Metrics Windows as wide as you can. The spacing is very wide and open at these large sizes. Trust the numbers I have given you and make the type look evenly spaced. Just do the best you can. The smoother you make the spacing now the less kerning you'll need later. [Plus, word processors and browsers do not kern anyway.]

If a character begins to bother you, simply double-click on the Metrics window when that character is selected. This will open the outline window for that glyph so you can edit it. Difficult letter spacing glyphs [like the Jjs] should also be opened so that you can get the left sidebearing right. This will also be true of the g.

Metrics navigation shortcuts

We've mentioned a few in passing, but let's get them written down in one place.

Move from letter to letter

Tab to go to the right and Shift+Tab to go to the left. Tabbing keeps the same measurement level selected. So, to set the kerning, you can tab from letter to letter simply typing in the numbers you like (or adjusting with the Option+Arrow keys as seen below).

Move up or down within a letter

Use the arrow keys to move up or down to the three settings: left sidebearing, right sidebearing, & kerning.

Change emu measurements

Adjusting the numbers for the left sidebearing, right sidebearing, & kerning are done with the right and left arrow keys while holding down the Option key. That changes the numbers up or down by one emu. Adding the Shift key makes the changes ten emus at a time.

Adding special characters

Checking characters which cannot be typed like the Euro or OpenType glyphs like b.sc requires that you add a slash before, as in /Euro or /b.sc. If you need (or use) Unicode numbers, add a backslash before the number.

Go through the entire text file to kern: You will be tempted to cut it short, but don't do it. All of the text in the kerning file is there for a reason. As you go through keep carefully observing the lettershapes themselves. The normal words are added into the copy to keep your eye calibrated to the normal letterspacing you have set for the font. Use them for your standard.

It is very easy to gradually get tighter and tighter (or looser and looser) as you go through the kerning process. If you find you are adding many more kerning pairs that you expect, check and make sure you aren't trying to tighten or loosen the basic letterspacing with excessive kerning pairs.

Some letterspacing tips

We've mentioned some of this already, but these things are so crucial the repetition is good. You need to take this seriously. In addition, you must remember that this is a "training of the eye" skill. I hope you remember when you began drawing. I recall my shock when I realized what I actually saw was so different from what I thought I saw. When I started setting type I couldn't tell Garamond from Times.

The same thing is true with letterspacing and kerning. When you start you will need to look closely to even see the issues. After a while, poor spacing will be like a slap in the face. Start examining the things you see printed—looking for obviously bad spacing and especially poor kerning.

Very quickly you will be able to instantly recognize anything done in a program which does not support kerning [like anything done in Office]. This is the main reason why projects done in Word look so unprofessional. As you train your eye in this way, your letterspacing in Fontographer will get better and better.

> ❦ Letterspace before doing any kerning: Adjusting sidebearings after you start kerning usually causes a major mess. So much of your kerning

is based on the basic letterspacing that it really must be finished before you start kerning.

- ❦ Save a copy of the font to use for your Web fonts before you begin kerning

Kerning adds to file size and most Web font distributors want very small fonts. Generate TrueType file with hints.

- ❦ Carefully distinguish between letter spacing and kerning pairs

For example, I was just spacing a new font I am working on to replace my current text font: Contenu. As usual, I was bothered by the spacing of pairs like ha he ho, ma me mo, na ne no. It seems like I am always adding kerning for those pairs. As I looked carefully, I could finally see that the lack of a corner on the shoulder of these letters always leaves a little extra white space. I decided to make the right sidebearing of the h, m, and n 15 emus less. This solved the problem through the font. So, these nine pairs are not a kerning problem but a letter spacing problem.

- ❦ Build your ligatures *after* your basic spacing is set

As mentioned earlier, the internal spacing of your ligatures is based on your normal letterspacing. You need to have decided what that is before you start building ligatures.

- ❦ The space character is smaller than you think

Moye suggests the width of the i for this. That sounds seems to work well. He is correct in stating that word spaces are much smaller than you think. You fix this after all your auto spacing and auto kerning is completed. Watch your word spacing in your testing of the font. If you see problems, start with the lowercase i width. (Open the space outline window and add the lower case i component. This will set the spacing. Then delete the i.)

Stick with it. You will be amazed at how much better your fonts look when they are spaced well.

Appendix B: Dealing with OpenType & Resources

In two words, it's confusing. Fontographer really does not deal well with OpenType at all. Having said that, if you have a feature file, you can use it. As you noticed for CushingTwo, the template came with a .fea file that you linked to in the font info dialog box. Fontographer will use that feature file to build your OpenType font when you generate it.

No way to edit that feature file

Fontographer does not provide any way to edit the file. You must have one already built and use it. There is no interface within Fontographer to do that.

Fontographer's manual has good help

I learned a lot about OpenType feature writing by reading Fontographer's manual. I will use it to improve my feature files which I write in FontLab. FontLab has an excellent panel for writing OpenType feature files. I will gradually add templates with feature files to my Website. If you have any specific needs, you can email me at: david@bergsland.org. But I am not a good code writer, so I will have limitations in what I can do. If you have feature files you want to share, I will be happy to add them to the hackberry-fonts.com site.

Resources available

I've already mentioned the template we used to start Poniard and the one used for CushingTwo. You can find links for each of them on the Fontographer page of the Hackberry Font Foundry Website (www.hackberry-fonts.com). You will find a growing list of resources there (like the kerning text file). If you think of any other resource you want to add to the page or which you want me to create, just drop me an email at david@bergsland.org and we'll talk about it.

Index

www.ingramcontent.com/pod-product-compliance
Lightning Source LLC
Chambersburg PA
CBHW051232050326
40689CB00007B/901